EXAMINING REASONING

CLASSROOM TECHNIQUES TO HELP STUDENTS PRODUCE AND DEFEND CLAIMS

EXAMINING REASONING

CLASSROOM TECHNIQUES TO HELP STUDENTS PRODUCE AND DEFEND CLAIMS

Tracy L. Ocasio and Robert J. Marzano

With Ria A. Schmidt and Deana Senn

1400 Centrepark Blvd, Suite 1000
West Palm Beach, FL 33401
717-845-6300

email: pub@learningsciences.com
learningsciences.com

Printed in the United States of America

20 19 18 17 16   1 2 3 4

FSC
www.fsc.org
MIX
Paper from
responsible sources
FSC® C011935

Publisher's Cataloging-in-Publication Data
Ocasio, Tracy L.
   Examining reasoning : classroom techniques to help students produce and defend claims / Tracy L. Ocasio [and] Robert J. Marzano.
      pages cm. – (Essentials for achieving rigor series)
   ISBN: 978-1-941112-06-9 (pbk.)
1. Reasoning—Study and teaching. 2. Critical thinking—Study and teaching. 3. Thought and thinking—Study and teaching. 4. Cognitive learning. 5. Academic achievement. I. Marzano, Robert J. II. Title.
   BF441 . O43 2015
   153.4—dc23
                    [2014939271]

MARZANO CENTER

Essentials for Achieving Rigor SERIES

The *Essentials for Achieving Rigor* series of instructional guides helps educators become highly skilled at implementing, monitoring, and adapting instruction. Put it to practical use immediately, adopting day-to-day examples as models for application in your own classroom.

Books in the series:

Identifying Critical Content: Classroom Techniques to Help Students Know What Is Important

Examining Reasoning: Classroom Techniques to Help Students Produce and Defend Claims

Recording & Representing Knowledge: Classroom Techniques to Help Students Accurately Organize and Summarize Content

Examining Similarities & Differences: Classroom Techniques to Help Students Deepen Their Understanding

Processing New Information: Classroom Techniques to Help Students Engage with Content

Revising Knowledge: Classroom Techniques to Help Students Examine Their Deeper Understanding

Practicing Skills, Strategies & Processes: Classroom Techniques to Help Students Develop Proficiency

Engaging in Cognitively Complex Tasks: Classroom Strategies to Help Students Generate & Test Hypotheses across Disciplines

Creating & Using Learning Targets & Performance Scales: How Teachers Make Better Instructional Decisions

Organizing for Learning: Classroom Techniques to Help Students Interact within Small Groups

Dedication

To Timothy Schell, a great father who had a heart for the success of all children, and Dion Workman, my best friend.

—Tracy L. Ocasio

Table of Contents

Visit www.learningsciences.com/bookresources to download materials from this book.

Acknowledgments

Learning Sciences International would like to thank the following reviewers:

Amanda J. Bush
Reading Teacher
Fort Clarke Middle School
Gainesville, Florida

George E. Goodfellow
2008 Rhode Island State Teacher of
   the Year
Scituate High School
North Scituate, Rhode Island

Dorothy Goff Goulet
2009 US Department of Defense
   Teacher of the Year
Ramstein High School
Ramstein Air Base, Germany

Mary Lu Hutchins
Ohio County Public Schools
Wheeling, West Virginia

Leah Lechleiter-Luke
Spanish Teacher and Global Scholars
   Coordinator
Mauston High School
Mauston, Wisconsin

Jessica Pack
2014 California Teacher of the Year
James Workman Middle School
Cathedral City, California

Terrie L. Ponder
Rome City Schools
Rome, Georgia

Aaron Sitze
National Board Certified English
   Teacher
Oregon High School
Oregon, Illinois

About the Authors

TRACY L. OCASIO, EdD, was a successful Principal and Assistant Superintendent for Curriculum and Instruction prior to working at LSI. She has more than twenty-five years in education including experience as a teacher of English as a second language, a reading specialist, an English teacher, an instructional support teacher, an elementary teacher, and a preschool teacher. Ms. Ocasio relates her early childhood through twelfth-grade experience to our work and incorporates this background into the blogs she writes for the Marzano Center. Her professional career includes teaching at the undergraduate and graduate levels as well as working as a crisis intervention/emergency services unit supervisor. She received a master's degree in public administration and education as well as doctorates in reading and language development and educational leadership.

ROBERT J. MARZANO, PhD, is CEO of Marzano Research Laboratory and Executive Director of the Learning Sciences Marzano Center for Teacher and Leader Evaluation. A leading researcher in education, he is a speaker, trainer, and author of more than 150 articles on topics such as instruction, assessment, writing and implementing standards, cognition, effective leadership, and school intervention. He has authored over 30 books, including *The Art and Science of Teaching* (ASCD, 2007) and *Teacher Evaluation That Makes a Difference* (ASCD, 2013).

RIA A. SCHMIDT, PhD, has experience as a teacher and administrator, with experience in creating/presenting professional development sessions on a variety of topics; guiding district transitions from traditional to standards-based education; and, coordinating use of assessments and data for informing instruction.

DEANA SENN, MSSE, is the Lead Content Developer and a Senior Staff Developer for Learning Sciences Marzano Center. Her experience spans the United States and Canada in both rural and urban settings. Ms. Senn received her BS from Texas A&M University and MS from Montana State University.

Introduction

This guide, *Examining Reasoning: Classroom Techniques to Help Students Produce and Defend Claims,* is intended as a resource for improving a specific element of instructional practice—teaching students how to produce and defend claims derived from two sources: 1) their own reasoning as it occurs in classroom discussions and is evidenced in their writing; and 2) the logic of information presented in print, processes, and procedures. The phrase *examining reasoning* encompasses these two cognitive processes.

Your motivation to incorporate this strategy into your instructional toolbox may have come from a personal desire to improve your instructional practice through the implementation of a research-based set of strategies (such as those found in the Marzano instructional framework) or a desire to increase the rigor of the instructional strategies you implement in your classroom so that students meet the expectations of demanding standards such as the Common Core State Standards, Next Generation Science Standards, C3 Framework for Social Studies State Standards, or state standards based on or influenced by the College and Career Readiness Anchor Standards.

This guide is designed to help teachers of all grade levels and subjects improve their performance of a single instructional strategy. Narrowing your focus on a specific strategy, such as examining reasoning, will enable you to more fully understand its complexities to intentionally improve your instruction. Armed with deeper knowledge and practical instructional techniques, you will be able to intentionally plan, implement, monitor, adapt, reflect, and ultimately improve upon the execution of this element of your instructional practice. An individual seeking to become an expert displays distinctive behaviors, as explained by Marzano and Toth (2013):

- breaks down the specific skills required to be an expert

- focuses on improving those particular critical skill chunks (as opposed to easy tasks) during practice or day-to-day activities

- receives immediate, specific, and actionable feedback, particularly from a more experienced coach

- continually practices each critical skill at more challenging levels with the intention of mastering it, giving far less time to skills already mastered

This series of guides will support each of the above-listed behaviors, with a focus on breaking down the specific skills required to be an expert and giving day-to-day practical suggestions to enhance these skills.

Building on the Marzano Instructional Model

This series is based on the Marzano instructional framework, which is grounded in research and provides educators with the tools they need to connect instructional practice to student achievement. The series uses key terms that are specific to the Marzano model of instruction. See Table 1, Glossary of Key Terms.

Table 1: Glossary of Key Terms

Term	Definition
CCSS	Common Core State Standards is the official name of the standards documents developed by the Common Core State Standards Initiative (CCSSI), the goal of which is to prepare students in the United States for college and career.
CCR	College and Career Readiness Anchor Standards are broad statements that incorporate individual standards for various grade levels and specific content areas.
Desired result	The intended result for the student(s) due to the implementation of a specific strategy.
Monitoring	The act of checking for evidence of the desired result of a specific strategy while the strategy is being implemented.
Instructional strategy	A category of techniques used for classroom instruction that has been proven to have a high probability of enhancing student achievement.
Instructional technique	The method used to teach and deepen understanding of knowledge and skills.
Content	The knowledge and skills necessary for students to demonstrate standards.
Scaffolding	A purposeful progression of support that targets cognitive complexity and student autonomy to reach rigor.
Extending	Activities that move students who have already demonstrated the desired result to a higher level of understanding.

The educational pendulum swings widely from decade to decade. Educators move back and forth between prescriptive checklists and step-by-step lesson plans to approaches that encourage instructional autonomy with minimal regard for the science of teaching and need for accountability. Two practices are often missing from both of these approaches to defining effective instruction: 1) specific statements of desired results, and 2) solid research-based connections. The Marzano instructional framework provides a comprehensive system that details what is required from teachers to develop their craft using research-based instructional strategies. Launching from this solid instructional foundation, teachers will then be prepared to merge that science with their own unique, yet effective, instructional style, which is the art of teaching.

Examining Reasoning: Classroom Techniques to Help Students Produce and Defend Claims will help you grow into an innovative and highly skilled teacher who is able to implement, scaffold, and extend instruction to meet a range of student needs.

Essentials for Achieving Rigor

This series of guides details essential classroom strategies to support the complex shifts in teaching that are necessary for an environment where academic rigor is a requirement for all students. The instructional strategies presented in this series are essential to effectively teach the CCSS, the Next Generation Science Standards, or standards designated by your school district or state. They require a deeper understanding, more effective use of strategies, and greater frequency of implementation for your students to demonstrate the knowledge and skills required by rigorous standards. This series includes instructional techniques appropriate for all grade levels and content areas. The examples contained within are grade-level specific and should serve as models and launching points for application in your own classroom.

Your skillful implementation of these strategies is essential to your students' mastery of the CCSS or other rigorous standards, no matter the grade level or subject matter you are teaching. Other instructional strategies covered in the Essentials for Achieving Rigor series, such as identifying critical content and engaging students in cognitively complex tasks, exemplify the cognitive complexity needed to meet rigorous standards. Taken as a package, these strategies may at first glance seem quite daunting. For this reason, the series focuses on just one strategy in each guide.

Examining Reasoning

One of the more challenging instructional undertakings for 21st century educators is teaching students how to examine and self-regulate their own thinking processes (reasoning) as well as critically evaluate the logic of presented content they encounter in the form of class discussions, various media formats, and content texts. These two facets of *examining reasoning* are cognitively complex skills. You sometimes may find them to be difficult to execute in your own life, and they are inarguably challenging to teach to students. You are not alone if you feel this way. In a study of the frequency of various observed content strategies, fewer than 2% of observed instructional episodes contained opportunities for students to engage with new content by either learning how to think more logically and critically from direct instruction about reasoning *or* applying reasoning to content texts and discussions (Marzano & Toth, 2014).

These findings are not surprising when you consider the many roadblocks to teaching students how to produce and defend claims by examining their own reasoning or the logic of presented information, processes, and procedures. These challenges include:

- extensive academic vocabulary and concepts that must be mastered by both teacher and students

- lessons that must be designed to show students how to engage in cognitive processes not readily understood by students

- instruction that must be married to rigorous content standards

- curricula and textbooks that may not support the instruction of critical thinking skills

- extensive teacher preparation and practice time that may not always be allocated

- extensive classroom instructional time that may not always be available

Here are some guidelines to use as an on-ramp to effective implementation:

- Become familiar with the academic vocabulary associated with the content. Select student-friendly definitions to consistently use in your teaching, and then begin introducing and explicitly teaching these terms to students.

- Seek opportunities to examine and evaluate your own reasoning techniques in order to prepare for thinking aloud for your students.

- Engage in periods of reflection during which you evaluate the logic of information you hear in news broadcasts or talk shows as well as articles you read in various online sources.

- Rehearse your thinking processes aloud using examples from current events or short opinion articles from newspapers. Take your thinking to your classroom and share it in think-alouds with students.

- Provide students with multiple opportunities to practice this strategy with less demanding content to scaffold their learning experiences. Your ultimate goal is to effectively implement this strategy throughout the lessons you design so that your students will intentionally examine the reasoning that occurs in class discussions, while reading content, and during the writing of reports and essays.

The Effective Implementation of Examining Reasoning

There are multiple ways to effectively help students produce and defend claims by examining their own reasoning or considering the logic of presented information, processes, and procedures. Two aspects of effective implementation are found in Parts I and II of this guide.

In Part I, you will learn to design lessons and structure activities to show students how to examine errors in their own logic or identify limitations in the logic of presented information.

In Part II, you will learn how to design learning opportunities to show students how to support a claim or assertion with evidence and evaluate the claims and evidence of others. Such claims might be those made by students or claims encountered in textbooks, resource materials, classroom discussions, or various media.

There are several teacher actions or behaviors associated with an effective implementation of examining reasoning. They are listed here to illustrate the variety and complexity of ways you can show your students how to identify and articulate errors in logic and reasoning or the structure of an argument as well as explain new insights resulting from this analysis:

- identifying critical content for examination by students

- teaching students how to examine and analyze information for errors—or informal fallacies in content or in their own reasoning— through directly instructing, modeling, and facilitating

- providing ongoing opportunities for students to identify common errors in logic

- teaching students how to state and support a claim with grounds, backing, and qualifiers through directly instructing, modeling, and facilitating

- providing ongoing opportunities for students to state and support a claim with grounds, backing, and qualifiers

- teaching students how to examine and analyze the strength of support presented for a claim in content or in their own reasoning through directly instructing, modeling, and facilitating

- teaching students how to analyze errors so they can identify more efficient ways to execute processes through directly instructing, modeling, and facilitating

- providing ongoing opportunities for students to learn how to support claims and assertions for those claims in relationship to the evidence

You no doubt noted the repetition of three terms: *directly instructing*, *modeling*, and *facilitating*. To learn and then teach how to examine reasoning requires knowledge about a substantial body of words—vocabulary you must first thoroughly understand, so that you and your students can use a common language to converse about reasoning. As the teacher, you may need to nail down more specific definitions for words that are familiar yet remain elusive when you try to define them in the context of this strategy. Then, you will have to determine the "what" and "how" of teaching this new language to students. Hence the need to teach students more directly.

In addition to teaching directly, also model the concepts and processes of reasoning. Modeling a cognitive process takes place when you think aloud to your students about how you are making decisions about whether your reasoning is sound and identifying any errors you might have made. As you persevere with direct instruction and modeling, your students will gradually become ready for a different kind of instruction: facilitating. Facilitating means that you will be thinking along with students and helping them develop their own ideas, rather than managing their thinking by overexplaining ideas, and telling them what to do and how to do it.

Finally, you must provide ongoing opportunities for students to engage in reasoning associated with the standards and content texts of your grade level or subject. Your goal, irrespective of grade level or content, is to gradually release the responsibility for logical reasoning to your students with the expectation that they will assume this responsibility in the future without prompting.

As you implement this strategy, you will inevitably make some mistakes along the way. However, forearmed with knowledge of the more common mistakes, you will be able to implement more effectively from the outset. Here are some of the common mistakes that can take teaching and therefore learning off course:

- The teacher doesn't identify and utilize content-related and standards-aligned instructional resources—for example, textbooks, trade books, other printed resources, or media.

- The teacher either doesn't know how to or doesn't take the time needed to integrate related instructional strategies that are essential to the implementation of this strategy.

- The teacher fails to provide the instruction necessary for students to acquire the reasoning process.

- The teacher doesn't model and think aloud for students—doing more telling than showing.

- The teacher doesn't give students enough opportunities to learn and practice challenging concepts—hurrying through lessons in order to "cover" material.

- The teacher doesn't give students enough "think time" to reason during classroom discussions.

Failing to Identify and Utilize Appropriate Materials

You may overlook the overriding goal of examining reasoning: to more deeply understand and retain content knowledge and procedures. The instructional techniques found in this guide are meant to be used in the context of rigorous content, not simply as a workbook activity to fill a class period. Endeavor to match instructional techniques with the most relevant and related content and standards.

Failing to Connect Related Instructional Strategies

You may miss the interdependence and cumulative effect of prerequisite instructional strategies. Consider a few of the many instructional strategies that pave the way for your students' success. You first identify the critical content. Then you chunk the critical content and preview it with students, leading them to process the content. Your goal is to skillfully blend these strategies in order to achieve the overall desired results. Failure to do this can leave you with the impression that your students are incapable of reasoning, while the problem may be gaps in your use of appropriate instructional strategies.

Failing to Provide the Necessary Instruction

Related to the previous mistake, this one arises when you assume that students will be able to execute a cognitively demanding process such as reasoning when you have not yet provided them with a lesson specifically designed to show them how to do it.

Failing to Show Rather Than Tell

This mistake often occurs when the carefully designed lesson referred to in the previous mistake does not include your modeling—thinking aloud for students—about how you execute this process when you are examining reasoning.

Failing to Provide Ongoing Opportunities

You may forget to provide daily opportunities for reasoning in your classroom. You make this mistake when you teach a lesson, process, or procedure once, and expect students to not only get it on the spot, but also remember it until the next class and automatically assume responsibility for doing it thereafter. Students need constant opportunities to learn from your modeling, from the reasoning of fellow students, and from a frequent examination of their own errors in reasoning.

Failing to Allow Students the Time to Process and Deepen Understanding

Examining reasoning cannot be rushed, especially when students are first learning how to stop and think about what they have said or heard. Time is needed for reflection, and when you fail to provide appropriate wait times during which students can process and deepen their understanding of a response or claim, you deprive them of an opportunity to consider the appropriateness of that claim and how it relates to what they have learned. They miss a valuable learning experience, one that will not only benefit them in the present moment but also serve to help them interact with an ever increasing body of subject-area knowledge. Students who can justify accurate responses develop a better understanding of content. Moreover, those given the opportunity to identify how reasoning yielded an inaccurate answer can also benefit tremendously from this type of analysis. With sufficient guidance and wait time to identify *why* an answer was inaccurate, students can reconsider what they thought they knew of the topic, reason through to an accurate understanding, and identify where the inaccuracy occurred.

Monitoring for the Desired Result

Effective implementation includes more than just applying the strategy—it also includes checking for evidence of the desired result of the specific strategy. In other words, effective implementation of a strategy includes monitoring for the desired result of the strategy in real time. Monitoring, in the context of the Essentials for Achieving Rigor framework, is defined as *the act of checking for evidence of the desired result of a specific strategy while the strategy is being implemented.* Teachers use their observation to answer the question, did the students learn or master the information taught? In the context of the Marzano instructional framework, a more specific question is, was the desired result of the strategy achieved? The most elaborately planned lessons can be exercises in futility unless they begin with a sharp focus on standards and content, include intentional planning for the use of specific techniques, and are closely monitored by the teacher for the desired results.

The student outcome is always the focus of the desired result for an instructional strategy. Here the student outcome is that the students can examine their own reasoning or the logic in the information presented and then use that analysis to deepen their understanding of the content.

There are multiple ways to monitor for the desired result, and these may look similar for many aspects of using the strategy discussed in this guide. Below are some examples of evidence demonstrating that your students are able to examine reasoning:

1. Students can describe errors or informal fallacies in information.

2. Students can evaluate the efficiency of a process.

3. Students can explain the overall structure of an argument presented to support a claim.

4. Student artifacts indicate that students can identify errors in reasoning.

5. Student artifacts demonstrate that students can identify and take various perspectives.

6. Students can identify support for their perspectives using the appropriate evidence.

7. Students are able to identify the support behind multiple perspectives.

8. Students can identify the evidence used to support the claim of others in presented information.

Scaffolding and Extending Instruction to Meet Students' Needs

As you monitor for the desired result of each instructional technique, you will likely discover that some students are not able to examine reasoning, while others can readily demonstrate the desired result of the technique you have taught. Knowing this, you must adapt for the needs of your students. You must plan in advance for those who may need scaffolding or extending of learning opportunities.

There are three categories of support you can provide for students who need scaffolding:

1. Manipulating the difficulty level of content that is being taught (e.g., providing an easier reading level that contains the same content)

2. Breaking down the content into smaller chunks to make it more manageable

3. Giving students organizers or think sheets to clarify and guide their thinking through a task one step at a time (Dickson, Collins, Simmons & Kame'enui, 1998)

Within each technique described in the book, there are brief examples of ways to scaffold and extend instruction to meet the needs of your students. Scaffolding provides support that targets cognitive complexity and student autonomy to reach rigor. Extending moves students who have already demonstrated the desired result to a higher level of understanding.

Teacher Self-Reflection

As you gain expertise in teaching students how to examine not only their own reasoning but also the logic of others, reflect on what works and doesn't work to become more effective in your implementation of this strategy. Use the following set of reflection questions to guide you. The questions begin with simply reflecting on how to start the implementation process and then move to progressively more complex ways of helping students examine reasoning.

1. How can you incorporate some aspect of this strategy in your instruction?

2. How can you engage students in meaningful activities that require them to examine their own reasoning or the logic of information presented?

3. In addition to engaging students in examining their own reasoning or the logic of information presented, how can you monitor the extent to which students are deepening their content knowledge?

4. How might you adapt and create new techniques for helping students examine their reasoning, to address their unique needs and situations?

5. What are you learning about your students' reasoning abilities as you adapt and create new techniques?

Instructional Techniques to Help Students Examine Reasoning

There are many ways to help students examine either their own reasoning or the logic in presented information. These ways are called instructional techniques, and in the following pages you will find six of them. They are presented in two parts. Part I contains three techniques to teach students how to examine and evaluate their own reasoning, while Part II presents three techniques to show your students how to produce and defend claims.

Part I: Examining Logic in Reasoning

Instructional Technique 1: Using logic to examine a response

Instructional Technique 2: Examining errors and the accuracy of a response

Instructional Technique 3: Examining the efficiencies of multiple methods of problem solving

Part II: Supporting Claims or Assertions with Evidence

Instructional Technique 4: Producing and defending claims related to content

Instructional Technique 5: Identifying and analyzing claims in an author's work

Instructional Technique 6: Judging reasoning and evidence in an author's work

All of the techniques are similarly organized and include the following components:

- a brief introduction to the technique

- ways to effectively implement the technique

- common mistakes to avoid as you implement the technique

- examples and nonexamples from elementary and secondary classrooms using selected learning targets or standards from the various documents

- ways to monitor for the desired result

- ways to scaffold and extend instruction to meet the needs of students

PART I

EXAMINING LOGIC IN REASONING

As teachers, we yearn to have students in our classrooms who are logical and sensible, and whose thinking leads them to self-reflection and a deep desire to produce an accurate response. Those dreams are often disrupted on the first day of class when you realize that clear reasoning is not always present. However, reasoning can be taught. The three instructional techniques in Part I will give you a place to begin and hopefully inspire you to bring your own expertise and creativity to modifying and enhancing the techniques just ahead.

USING LOGIC TO EXAMINE A RESPONSE

Logic is a stepwise progression in thinking in which a statement or conclusion is supported by some type of evidence. The most basic questions you and your students must ask and answer as you implement this instructional technique are: *Does this answer make sense? Is my conclusion logical? What kind of evidence do I have to support this statement?*

Using logic to examine an assertion or response is a cognitive process in which you are constantly engaged. As you eat lunch in the teachers' lunchroom, you could likely find at least one or two assertions that contain faulty logic—errors in an individual's reasoning. Engaging colleagues in debate about their illogical thinking may not be a good option for a pleasing midday break; however, engaging students in similar types of discussions is precisely what you must do if you want to effectively implement using logic to examine reasoning in your classroom.

How to Effectively Implement Using Logic to Examine a Response

Here are some straightforward ways that you can introduce your students to using logic to examine a response. The students themselves or their classmates may give the response. With practice, they may even examine the logic of *your* statements and responses during instruction.

Directly Teach the Basic Vocabulary of Logic

Do not be intimidated by the vocabulary of logic. Synonyms such as *judgment* and *reasoning* are often used interchangeably with the term *logic*. However, the simplest way to say it may be how your grandmother reacted when addressing any situation that seemed to defy her logic: *Why can't you kids just use some common sense once in a while?*

Use the standards that inform your instruction, the grade level of your students, and any terms that are specific to your discipline to decide how you will frame the big ideas of logic: answers that make sense, conclusions that are logical, and evidence that supports these answers and conclusions. Develop a chart of student-friendly definitions to keep yourself and your students tied to a common language as you explore what it means to think logically and have a logical classroom.

Consider the following standards from the CCR Anchor Standards for Reading and Writing. They are loaded with the language of logic, and they appear at almost every grade level in some variation:

- Delineate and evaluate the argument and specific claims in a text, including the validity of the reasoning as well as the relevance and sufficiency of the evidence (CCR Anchor Standard, Reading, Standard #8).

- Write arguments to support claims in an analysis of substantive topics or texts using valid reasoning and relevant and sufficient evidence (CCR Anchor Standard, Writing, Standard #1).

- Draw evidence from literary or information texts to support analysis, reflection, and research (CCR Anchor Standard, Writing, Standard #9).

If you have not previously felt compelled to dig into the vocabulary and critical content of logic, these standards should provide the impetus.

If you teach math, also consider the Standards for Mathematical Practice. In particular:

- Reason abstractly and quantitatively.

- Construct viable arguments and critique the reasoning of others.

- Look for and make use of structure (CCSS, Mathematical Practice, Standards #2, 4, 7).

These mathematical practices are rich in requiring logic and reasoning and are applicable kindergarten through twelfth grade.

Directly Teach and Model the Four Types of Errors in Logic

Once you are comfortable with the language of logic and can discuss reasoning in an informal way with your students, begin to directly teach and model the four types of errors in logic: 1) errors of faulty logic, 2) errors of attack, 3) errors of weak reference, and 4) errors of misinformation. Once you and your students are briefed on all of the possible ways to think illogically, your classroom will never be the same.

Table 1.1 defines and exemplifies eight errors of faulty logic. This table is solely intended to familiarize you with the errors, refresh your memory regarding how they appear in typical arguments and assertions, and then help you keep track of the specific errors you teach directly to students. Choose those errors based on your assessment of students' knowledge, the demands of a required standard, and the instructional materials you expect students to process. Resist the temptation to prepare a handout, assign homework, or give a quiz containing all of the errors.

Table 1.1: Eight Errors of Faulty Logic

Error	Description	Example
Contradiction	Presenting conflicting information.	I am a vegetarian, but I always eat meat if it is offered to me at a party.
Accident	Basing an argument on an exception to a rule.	Smoking doesn't have anything to do with cancer. My grandma is 90, and she smokes a pack a day.
False cause	Confusing an order of events with causality or oversimplifying the reasons behind some event or occurrence.	A basketball player has a lucky pair of socks that he always wears, believing that the socks contribute to his good free-throw percentage.
Begging the question	Making a claim and then arguing for the claim by using statements that are the equivalent of the original claim.	Everybody knows smoking causes cancer. The smoke from cigarettes is a carcinogen.
Evading the issue	Changing the topic to avoid addressing the issue.	Mom asks Sally how she did on her algebra test, and Sally immediately changes the subject to the cute boy that sits behind her in algebra.

(continued on next page)

Table 1.1 (continued)

Error	Description	Example
Arguing from ignorance	Arguing that a claim is justified simply because its opposite has not been proven true.	A person argues that UFOs do not exist because there's no proof that they do.
Composition	Asserting something about a whole that is true of only its parts.	A person asserts that all police officers use excessive force because one officer has used excessive force.
Division	Asserting about all of the parts something that is generally, but not always, true of the whole.	A person asserts that a particular news reporter is liberal because all reporters are liberal.

Adapted from Marzano (2007).

The following table defines and exemplifies the second category of errors you may encounter anywhere—while at a faculty meeting, reading the newspaper, watching your favorite news panel, reading your students' essays, or engaging your students in class discussion. Once again, this table is solely intended to familiarize you with the errors and refresh your memory regarding how they appear in typical arguments and assertions. At some point you may wish to prepare a handout for your students, but keep it simple.

Table 1.2: Errors of Attack

Error	Description	Example
Poisoning the well	Being so committed to a position that opposing positions are ignored.	I don't really care what the research says about the importance of vaccinating children. I know for a fact that vaccinations are dangerous.
Arguing against the person	Rejecting a claim using derogatory facts (however real or imagined) about the person making the claim.	I have a difficult time believing anything she says about global warming. Did you know that she flunked out of college?
Appealing to force	Using threats to establish the validity of a claim.	I could have you fired. The board president is a close friend.

Adapted from Marzano (2007).

Errors of weak reference are described and exemplified in the following table. These are especially important for students to understand before they begin using the Internet as a source for defending claims they have made in class discussions and written work.

Table 1.3: Errors of Weak Reference

Error	Description	Example
Sources that reflect bias	Accepting information that supports what we already believe to be true or rejecting information that goes against what we believe to be true.	I only read that National Enquirer because their reporters always give you the straight scoop on what's happening in the world.
Sources that lack credibility	Using a source that is not reputable for a given topic.	Well, I trust the salesperson at the health food store. She is an expert on how to lower high blood pressure.
Appealing to authority	Invoking authority as the last word on an issue.	I know you don't agree with the school policy, but the board of education is the last word on this issue.
Appealing to people	Using authors, texts, or speakers showing the popularity of a decision to support a claim.	I feel quite sure about this curriculum decision. Many of the best and biggest districts are using it.
Appealing to emotion	Using a sad story as proof for a claim.	I heard about a woman whose daughter died because her new health policy refused to honor the prescriptions she needed to live.

Adapted from Marzano (2007) and Marzano, Boogren, Kanold-McIntyre, and Pickering (2012).

The following table defines and exemplifies two common errors of misinformation. Television and Internet reporting are rife with them. The pressure on digital reporters is intense, and articles are often posted without fact checking. Furthermore, facts are often shifting as citizens who are part of what's happening become part of the reporting. These errors of misinformation must be directly taught prior to any activity involving searching for information to defend claims. You will have no trouble finding authentic examples of errors of misinformation in schools and communities.

Table 1.4: Errors of Misinformation

Error	Description	Example
Confusing the facts	Using information that appears factual but has been changed to the extent that it is no longer accurate.	Telling a news story with key details missing from the description.
Misapplying a concept or generalization	Wrongly applying a concept or generalization to support a claim.	Believing that individuals who lose a civil case should go to jail.

Adapted from Marzano (2007).

Common Mistakes

Showing students how to use logic in their academic reasoning and writing is challenging. There will be many instances in which students' responses contain so many types of illogical thinking that you won't know where to begin with your instruction. Consider these common mistakes:

- The teacher uses examples during instruction that are too complex for students to understand.

- The teacher doesn't provide adequate time for students to think about responses.

- The teacher continues to identify and analyze errors for students rather than releasing the responsibility to students who could and should be thinking for themselves.

- The teacher consistently allows students to explain or describe an error without first identifying it by name.

- The teacher asks students to identify errors without requiring them to provide an explanation of why their responses were incorrect.

Examples and Nonexamples of Examining Logic in the Classroom

Following are two examples (one elementary and one secondary) and their corresponding nonexamples illustrating how students are learning how to examine logic in their responses. As you read them, think about the experiences you have had in the classroom. Consider the common mistakes and note how the example teacher avoids them and the nonexample teacher misses the mark by making one of the previously described common mistakes.

Elementary Example of Using Logic

In this example, the teacher is helping her third-grade students use logic to demonstrate their understanding of a read-aloud text, *The Little Red Hen Makes a Pizza* (Sturges, 2002). She has previously used this text as a way to model making logical inferences. They have also been working on that skill in their daily independent reading. Today, she is specifically focused on helping her students become more intentional about examining their reasoning as they respond to her questions or prompts found on think sheets they complete while reading text.

Boys and girls, I have been listening very carefully to the answers you give to questions I ask or the answers you write on your think sheets while you're reading or working cooperatively in your groups. Sometimes your answers just don't make sense. They are incorrect. Now, I could just tell you, "Your answer is wrong," and ask someone else for the right answer. But, if I did that, I wouldn't be a very good teacher. I want to show you how to think about your answer with all of your superpower thinking skills and figure out on your own that it isn't the correct answer. We're going to play a game and ask ourselves the question, "Does my answer make sense to me?"

If you say "yes," I want to know the reason why you think so. You will have to give me an explanation. If you say "no," then you'll have to tell me why the answer doesn't make sense to you.

The teacher briefly recaps the story for students, hitting the highlights that show the little red hen giving in to her desire to make a pizza. Over the course of the story, she makes three trips to the grocery store for the ingredients she needs to make the pizza. During these repeated trips, she also fills her shopping cart with multiple items irrelevant to preparing pizza.

The question the teacher has posed for her students is this: "Do the actions of the little red hen make sense to you? Yes or no." She asks for a volunteer: "Who wants to do a sample with me to show the rest of the class how this works?"

Jose volunteers and quickly answers, "No, they don't make any sense to me at all." The teacher asks the students to raise their hands if they think Jose is correct. The class is somewhat divided, not quite sure about where the teacher is going. The teacher asks Jose why he decided that the red hen's actions didn't make sense. "You have to give me one commonsense reason why."

Jose thinks for a second or two and admits that he has no idea why he decided "no." The teacher suggests that he must have been thinking about *something* when he said "no." Jose says, "Well, it didn't make sense to me that she didn't make a list of all the things she needed to make her pizza before she went to the store."

Someone else volunteers another opinion: "It didn't make sense to me that when she got to the store she just wandered around and bought all this stuff that didn't have any connection to her pizza."

"Well, this whole book doesn't make any sense to me," offers Emily. The teacher wraps up this discussion with a reminder that from now on when they are answering questions or writing answers, they will be expected to take time to think if their answer makes sense. And, further, they will be expected to explain why.

Elementary Nonexample of Using Logic

Let us consider a nonexample of using logic based on the same grade level and instructional materials as the example. The nonexample teacher used the same text. However, after she introduced the question—and while her students were disengaged—she wrote down all of the answers and explanations on an overhead projector, even though they had processed the text together and were having great success with making inferences. This nonexample teacher failed to expect her students to do the thinking.

Secondary Example of Using Logic

This example features a social-studies class. The content that students are expected to master involves particular aspects of President Richard Nixon's leadership while in office. To guide students in using logic to complete their assignment, the teacher focuses on this learning target: Delineate and evaluate the argument and specific claims in a text, assessing whether the reasoning is valid and the evidence is relevant and sufficient; identify false statements and fallacious reasoning. (CCSS ELA & Literacy, Reading–Informational Text Grades 9–10, Standard #8). He keeps this standard in mind as he plans his lessons, but for this lesson, using Technique 1, he is facilitating his students' ability to evaluate their own and their classmates reasoning as they read and discuss in small groups certain aspects of Nixon's presidency.

> Class, we have been learning about various errors in reasoning. Today, you are going to apply what you know about errors in reasoning to evaluate your own thinking and reasoning as well as the thinking of your classmates.

In the past, the teacher has divided students into small groups and assigned each group a particular aspect of a topic to evaluate. In the lesson today, the teacher chooses not to use this jigsaw form of cooperative learning where students teach each other critical content. Rather, he wants them to focus on the reasoning they are using to draw a conclusion, thereby making a claim about one aspect of Nixon's presidency: foreign relations. The students in each group review the information they previously read in their textbook as well as consult a number of primary and secondary documents. After all groups make a decision regarding their findings, a reporter from each one presents the group's finding and rationale for its claim to the class.

At this point, one group is chosen to discuss and defend its reasoning regarding Nixon's foreign relations achievement. Students in the rest of the class are encouraged to identify any examples of faulty logic, contradictory information, or potential sources of bias not considered by the group currently defending its conclusion. The teacher does not explain or "think" for the students at this point in the lesson. Students take ownership of the discussion with a high level of involvement from the majority of students.

Secondary Nonexample of Using Logic

The nonexample secondary teacher begins his lesson the same way, and his students do a creditable job of reading and answering the questions.

However, the nonexample teacher fails to push students to the level expected in the standard by not requiring the students to assess the reasoning of their own group and others as they draw conclusions about Nixon's leadership.

Determining If Students Can Use Logic to Examine Reasoning

Always make time to monitor whether students are able to use logic to examine their own reasoning. To find out how well they are able to articulate their reasons for thinking a particular way, assemble a toolkit of tasks designed to fit your grade or content area. Here are some ways that you can monitor your students' abilities to examine reasoning:

- Students indicate their answer to a question by displaying one of two response cards: *Yes* or *No*. You can quickly see which students have made incorrect choices, and follow up by probing their thinking.

- Students keep journals or learning logs in which they write entries about their thinking relative to a specific problem or question.

- Students respond chorally. The teacher notes the students who respond incorrectly and makes a mental note that these students need more opportunities to respond. The teacher ensures that all students respond and can be heard.

Use the following student proficiency scale for using logic to examine reasoning.

Table 1.5: Student Proficiency Scale for Using Logic to Examine Reasoning

Emerging	Fundamental	Desired Result
Students can define some of the errors of reasoning, but are unable to identify the errors in either their own thinking and writing or the academic work of classmates.	Students can define many of the errors of reasoning, identify some of them in their own reasoning and writing, and evaluate reasoning of the academic work of classmates.	Students can successfully define and identify errors in the context of their own thinking and writing. They are able to offer simple examples of the most common reasoning errors. They are able to apply this skill in the context of their classmates' reasoning and writing as well.

Scaffold and Extend Instruction to Meet Students' Needs

As you become more skilled at teaching students the various errors in logic and how to identify them, you will no doubt spot students who need different approaches than you have provided thus far. Some students need support, or scaffolding, that takes them from where they are to where they need to be. Other students need to be challenged further, so you must extend the ways in which you expect them to use logic in their work.

Scaffolding

When students are struggling to understand specific errors in logic or figuring out why their own reasoning is faulty, use more concrete examples to illustrate the errors. Political cartoons, advertisements, and editorials are excellent sources for helping many students gain practice with considering logic. However, practical illustrations or examples are often more useful for students who have difficulties with abstract thinking. Use familiar examples, particularly those in narrative form. These illustrations can then be used to make connections to relevant content.

Graphic organizers are another option to use to help struggling students keep track of a logical progression in a narrative or an argument. For learners who benefit from nonlinguistic representations, graphic organizers that identify key points of support and their relationship help students sort the main ideas that an author is using to share his or her logic. They also make it easier for students to delineate the critical information from all the verbiage that can be distracting as students attempt to draw conclusions from fast-moving discussions.

Extending

Consider the following examples as ways to motivate more advanced students to further develop their higher-level thinking skills:

- Generate a set of examples for each of the reasoning errors and develop a matching game that could be used with students having difficulty with error identification.

- Develop a skit in which the participants deliberately use errors in reasoning while class members try to identify the errors.

Instructional Technique 2

EXAMINING ERRORS AND THE ACCURACY OF A RESPONSE

The first instructional technique helped your students become aware of a sizable body of various errors in reasoning and showed them how to identify some of those errors in their own reasoning. Instructional Technique 2 takes students to a higher level: expecting students to become conversant with a wider set of logic errors, giving students tools to identify whether a response is inaccurate, and subsequently providing them with ways to either correct an inaccurate response or provide a rationale for why a response is accurate.

How to Effectively Implement Examining Errors and the Accuracy of a Response

You have probably encountered a fair share of students who give wrong answers over and over again and are seemingly unable to figure out where they went wrong. The critical attribute of such students is that they jump to conclusions. They somehow miss the point of everything. Students like these need you to implement Instructional Technique 2. Here are some guidelines for designing instruction that can help them avoid jumping to conclusions.

Teach the Term: Jumping to Conclusions

All students can make reasoning errors if the content is difficult, they lack appropriate background knowledge, or they are working toward English proficiency. However, some students are just lazy thinkers. Rather than engaging in a discussion and following its logic, lazy thinkers hijack the discussion with excessive elaborations about their own experiences. These students jump to conclusions constantly.

Develop a set of questions that students can consult when they jump to a conclusion and produce a wrong answer. It may lead them to one of the eight types of errors in logic described in Instructional Technique 1. These questions will personalize the errors in logic so that students can more readily evaluate their own reasoning and identify the errors they make consistently. You will most likely have several reasons of your own to add to this list. Once you have identified all of the reasons your students make errors in reasoning, give them a copy of the following checklist to use to evaluate their own conclusions. Note that the common errors in logic have been reworded to make them more user friendly to students. Define specific terms for students as needed.

Top Ten Reasons Why Students Make Errors in Reasoning

1. I made an assumption that isn't accurate.

2. I didn't have enough information to draw the appropriate conclusion.

3. I had the wrong information to draw the appropriate conclusion.

4. I have a personal bias that is interfering with drawing the right conclusion.

5. I constantly evade the issue and go off topic, making it impossible for me to draw the right conclusion.

6. I think that if something happens once or twice, it must be true all the time.

7. I think that if two things occur together, one must have caused the other.

8. I refuse to consider the possibility that I might be wrong.

9. I make frequent derogatory statements about another person.

10. I rely more on emotion and force than logic and reason.

Use Authentic Examples with Students

Collect as many examples of errors in reasoning as you can from everyday life, newspapers, TV shows, or Internet sources. Use these examples to sensitize your students to the pervasive presence of unsound reasoning that surrounds them. Hold a month-long contest awarding students points or prizes for bringing in examples of errors in reasoning. The evidence they provide must be in the form of a video clip, a print copy of a news story, or an Internet web link where the example can be found.

Require Students to Provide Justification

Provide students with ongoing opportunities to explain their work, requiring them to provide a rationale for the steps taken. Standards in most states acknowledge the importance of students understanding the many ways to solve most problems or arrive at a resolution.

Anticipate Student Errors and Model Them in the Presentation of Content

Design your lessons to incorporate the common errors you anticipate students might make. Helping students become aware of common errors before they start an assignment can avoid common pitfalls. Develop a checklist of common errors that students can use to evaluate their work.

Common Mistakes

The most common mistakes you can make as you work toward effectively implementing this technique all relate to the opportunities students have to learn and practice this skill. There is a constant temptation in the interests of "covering the material" or "moving things along" to assume all of the responsibility for thinking in your classroom. Releasing responsibility to students for identifying their errors, figuring out how to correct their errors, and providing a rationale for why their response is correct is the key to enabling your students to become critical thinkers. Be aware of these common mistakes as you implement this technique:

- The teacher doesn't provide students with the constancy of instruction, practice, and accountability they must have to become logical thinkers.

- The teacher is too willing to accept careless thinking in the interest of moving on.

- The teacher doesn't insist that students explain how and why they arrived at a correct answer.

- The teacher doesn't hold students accountable for identifying an error before offering an explanation that describes or explains it.

- The teacher doesn't involve a wide range of students in answering questions and providing justification for answers, preferring to call only on students who always have the correct answer.

- The teacher uses examples that are too complex for students to analyze.

Examples and Nonexamples of Helping Students to Examine Errors and the Accuracy of Their Responses

Following are two examples (one elementary and one secondary) and their corresponding nonexamples of having students identify responses as inaccurate, explain how to correct them, and give a rationale for why the response is accurate. As you read the examples, think about the experiences you have had in your own classroom. Recall the common mistakes discussed previously, and note how the example teacher avoids making the mistakes and the nonexample teacher takes the class down the wrong path.

Elementary Example of Examining Errors

The example features an elementary teacher who is using two learning targets to guide her instruction:

- Make sense of problems and persevere in solving them.

- Reason abstractly and quantitatively (CCSS, Mathematical Practice, Standards #1, 2).

As in our earlier example at the elementary level, the teacher has introduced students to an important question in her classroom: *Does that make sense?* She has shown students several hands-on examples of things that do and don't make sense. She has gone so far as to introduce the term *logic*, explaining to students that when what they say or do makes sense they are using logic, a superpower thinking skill. In this example, she is taking the next step—expecting her students to use their superpower thinking skill of logic as they distinguish between attributes of shapes, then figure out if the way they sorted shapes is accurate.

> Boys and girls, I want you to use your superpower thinking skills to figure out if something makes sense to you. We are going to sort some shapes. I need your help to do that. When I point to you, quietly stand up and bring the shape I handed out with you. I will tell you where to stand. Every time we sort a shape, I want you to ask yourself and your partner, "Does this make sense?"

She directs four students to stand in the front of the room. Directing two students with triangles to one area and the students with the square and rectangle to another area, she asks the students to silently determine if they can figure out how she is sorting the shapes. She directs the students to talk to their partner and tell what they saw in the shapes the four students were holding. As the partners talk, she walks around and monitors their conversations. The teacher then asks a student to share what she and her partner decided about which attribute she is using to sort the shapes, while knowing from her monitoring that the group stated correctly that she is sorting by how many sides are on the shape.

Next, the teacher tells the students she's going to sort a few more shapes. At this point, the teacher makes an error as she sorts, adding an octagon to the four-sided shape group. She asks the question she wants her students to answer to each other, "Does this shape make sense in the group I placed it?" She directs the students to talk to their partners, giving them an opportunity to identify the error. Next, the teacher selects a different pair of partners to share their answer. One of the partners tells the teacher that she was incorrect when sorting the shape, and the teacher *reminds the student to explain why.* She then selects a student from the class to correct her error and further explain why the correction is right. Meanwhile, she directs the other students to give a "thumbs up" if they agree with the solution. She knows that students will often get a correct answer by accident and so need to be able to explain why an answer makes sense.

Elementary Nonexample of Examining Errors
The teacher in our elementary nonexample of examining errors works with sorting shapes similar to those of the example teacher. However, she

doesn't expect students to identify errors and explain why a certain shape placement is incorrect. The lesson focuses only on sorting shapes correctly, failing to give students opportunities to learn from the errors the teacher intentionally creates by explaining why a shape placement is wrong.

Secondary Example of Using Logic

In this secondary example of using logic, a high school physics teacher has planned a lesson designed around the following learning target: Construct viable arguments and critique the reasoning of others. (CCSS, Mathematical Practice, Standard #3)

The standard goes on to explain that mathematically proficient students are also able to compare the effectiveness of two plausible arguments, distinguish correct logic or reasoning from that which is flawed, and—if there is a flaw in an argument—explain what it is.

> Class, you have ten minutes to work the problem I've put on the SMART Board. It's similar to those you will be encountering on your Advanced Placement physics exam in the spring. As you work through the problem, be aware of the reason you selected the particular method you did.

Next, the teacher displays the problems completed two different ways and their corresponding point values (one receiving fewer points and one receiving more points). Her objective now is to facilitate discussion among the various student groups to help them determine the rationale for choosing the method they did as well as the rationale for the point allocation of the two methods.

She then asks students to work together in their small, already formed groups and discuss their work, directing them to arrive at a consensual answer regarding the questions. She asks the students in the first group to come to the board and share their consensual answer. The remaining groups are then asked to identify the differences in their own work compared to the work displayed.

All students are required to evaluate their work and write a rationale for the steps they took to arrive at an answer. They are required to identify why they would change the answer they derived.

*Secondary Nonexample of Examining
Errors and Assessing Accuracy*

The teacher in this nonexample is known by parents and students to be much "easier" than our example teacher. She generally does not hold students accountable for explanations about *why* they have chosen a certain method or *why* they would make specific changes to their methodology. Those students who chose the better method may not even be able to articulate why they selected that method, and those who got incorrect answers, no matter what method they selected, are left to figure it out on their own.

Determining If Students Can Examine Reasoning by Identifying Errors and Accuracy

You will only know that your instruction has achieved the desired result if your students are able to explain why they have selected a certain method or, as in the elementary example, decided on the most appropriate way to complete a pattern. To that end, two things have to happen:

1. Your students must engage in some kind of activity requiring them to demonstrate that they are certain of the accuracy of their response and can explain why that is so *or*, if their response contains an error, how they will correct that error.

2. You, the teacher, must engage in some kind of monitoring action, such as reading students' learning logs, to determine that your students really are assessing their accuracy and examining their errors.

This two-step process ensures accountability. It lets you know whether what you are doing is helping your students become logical thinkers.

Consider the following suggestions for monitoring:

● As students are working on a problem, walk around the room and read over their shoulders to ensure they are on the right track.

- As students discuss their reasoning in small groups, walk around and listen to the conversations.

- Make notes in your lesson plans about various ways students have explained their reasoning. Use this information to make changes in your next lesson.

The scale describes the levels of performance on the first technique: *helping students examine the accuracy of their response*. It provides identifiers for two types of reasoning: how to identify whether a response is incorrect and explain how to correct it, and how to identify whether a response is correct and provide a rationale for why it is correct.

Table 2.1: Student Proficiency Scale for Examining Errors and Determining the Accuracy of a Response

Emerging	Fundamental	Desired Result
Students can identify that a response is inaccurate but cannot explain why the response is inaccurate. Students can identify that a response is accurate but cannot explain why the response is accurate.	Students can identify that a response is inaccurate but can offer only limited information as to why the response is inaccurate. Students can identify that a response is accurate but can offer only limited information as to why the response is accurate.	Students can identify that a response is inaccurate and explain how to correct the inaccurate response. Students can identify that a response is accurate and provide a rationale for why the response is accurate.

Scaffold and Extend Instruction to Meet Students' Needs

When you come up against the challenge of students who find the content and skills difficult to master at the same pace as other students or encounter students that have already mastered a skill, you adapt. That means you scaffold or extend the instruction to meet the needs of different groups of students. Below are examples of both scaffolding and extending.

Scaffolding

When you are having difficulty with individuals or small groups of students who do not seem to grasp or remember the critical content from day to day, or even in the same day, try one of the following ways to adjust your instruction:

- Identify errors for students and then ask them to justify why a particular assertion or response is that type of error. When students can successfully justify, they can be transitioned to complete both steps in the reasoning process: identifying and justifying.

- Provide a list of critical attributes or conditions for each type of error. For example, when considering errors of accident (i.e., basing your argument on an exception to the rule), provide the following prompts as a scaffold: 1) What do you think the rule is? 2) Can you think of any exceptions to that rule? If the students can, their logic is faulty.

- Focus on one reasoning error at a time and lead students to generate as many examples as they can to illustrate that error. Focus on the errors that seem to crop up regularly in literary texts, in classroom interactions, or even during playground incidents.

Extending

Here are several examples of how to extend this particular instructional technique:

- Have students compare and contrast multiple types of errors or different examples of the same types of errors.

- Have students prepare multiple examples for different types of errors.

- Have students prepare a flowchart for the various steps they use to assess the accuracy of their answers.

EXAMINING THE EFFICIENCIES OF MULTIPLE METHODS OF PROBLEM SOLVING

The focus of this technique is showing students how to use logic to become more flexible and adaptable in how they solve problems. The problems can be mathematical, scientific, or related to one of the social sciences. The classroom examples presented for this instructional technique feature mathematics instruction. However, if you are a social studies teacher, there are ways to show your students how to consider the efficiency of solving problems in the social sciences. For example, compare quantitative research methods with those of qualitative research to determine which method will most readily provide the kind of information you need to solve the problem.

Scientific problem solving is known as the scientific method and usually involves the following steps: 1) observing, 2) asking questions, 3) generating hypotheses, 4) conducting an experiment to test the hypotheses, and 5) analyzing the data and drawing conclusions.

When you both encourage and expect students to examine and evaluate the efficiencies of various approaches available to them for solving particular problems, their reasoning capabilities will grow to meet the challenges of the new standards.

How to Examine Efficiencies of Multiple Ways to Solve a Problem

Following are two methods for teaching students how to examine the efficiencies of various problem-solving techniques.

Directly Teach One Method/Approach to Students

This approach is most appropriate for grade levels where students are being introduced to a new procedure or process to which they have had no previous instruction.

1. Identify a content-related and standards-aligned problem to be solved.

2. Model and demonstrate the problem-solving method using familiar examples and illustrations and/or less challenging texts. If appropriate, prepare a slide or transparency of the steps in the method—for example, the steps in solving a multiplication problem, using the scientific method, or developing a survey to collect data about a problem in the social sciences.

3. Give students copies of worked examples to consult during your lesson.

4. Provide organizers to help students keep track of their thinking, observations, and answers to questions.

5. Ask students to work through a new problem related to content with a partner.

6. Ask students to provide an explanation for the way they worked through the problem.

7. Ask students to give justification to support their reasoning or demonstrate why the solution they achieved is correct.

Use a Compare/Contrast Approach to Introduce Different Methods of Solving the Same Problem

1. Give students two problems and ask that each be worked through using a different method (typically a conventional method and a shortcut method that reduces the number of computations), showing the solutions side by side.

2. Pair students to discuss the solutions with a partner and answer questions about their discussion on a think sheet.

3. Ask questions focused on the efficiency and/or accuracy of each method.

4. Ask students to come up with specific instances of where one method would be preferred over another.

5. Ask students to give justification to support their decisions about the efficiency or accuracy of the two methods.

When students master this particular compare/contrast approach, use other variations to include 1) two different problems each solved the same way; or 2) two very similar problems, each solved the same way.

Common Mistakes

Learning from mistakes while trying to teach can be a frustrating experience. Knowing ahead of time where problems might arise will increase your likelihood of success in implementing this technique. Watch out for these common mistakes:

- The teacher uses examples or problems that may be too complex for students to analyze at their present level of expertise.

- The teacher is guilty of inadvertently telling students that there is just one way to solve the problem or that they had the correct answer but didn't solve the problem using the correct methodology.

- The teacher becomes impatient and resorts to telling students what they should be figuring out on their own.

- The teacher uses students' incorrect responses as examples to help other students understand rather than allowing the students in question to evaluate their own work, errors and all.

- The teacher provides the justification for students, unable to release the responsibility for thinking to the students.

- The teacher is excessively polite and overly reluctant to press students to explain any variance in the steps they may have taken.

- The teacher routinely accepts correct answers without pressing students to consider any inefficiencies in their methodology or explain how they arrived at their answer to avoid coming to a correct answer "by accident."

Examples and Nonexamples of Examining Efficiencies and Multiple Methods in the Classroom

Following are two examples (one elementary and one secondary) and their corresponding nonexamples of having students examine logic in their responses to examine the efficiencies of multiple methods. Both examples are from mathematics classes, but as you read, think about how they might translate into your grade level or content area. Consider the common mistakes and note how the example teacher avoids them and the nonexample teacher misses the mark.

Elementary Example of Examining the Efficiency of Multiple Methods

The first example illustrates how to use this instructional technique in a fourth-grade mathematics class. The teacher is addressing the following learning target: Developing understanding and fluency with multidigit multiplication (see also CCSS, Mathematics, Grade 4–Number & Operations in Base Ten, Standard 5).

During the weeks preceding this lesson, the teacher has directly taught three different methods of multiplication: the traditional method, the Partial Products Method, and the Lattice Method. Almost all of the students have demonstrated at least a basic proficiency in using the three methods, some with less fluency in their computational skills. However, the students are unable to talk or write about how these methods differ in their approaches and efficiency. They are gradually acquiring fluency with the multiplication of two 2-digit numbers, but they lack a deeper understanding of the processes that will be required on the state assessment. The teacher would like students to be able to produce a brief constructed response to answer prompts such as these: 1) Explain the process to find the product of 47×75 using the Partial Products Method of multiplication, 2) Explain the process to find the product of 47×75 using the Lattice Method of multiplication, and 3) Which method of multiplication is most efficient for you? Explain why.

Class, give me your best ready-to-learn posture. Excellent listening. During the past few weeks, we have been learning about the multiplication of two 2-digit numbers, and I have introduced you to three different ways to solve those problems. You're getting pretty good at using these methods to come up with answers. But that's not enough to do well on our state assessment. On the assessment, you will be asked to explain how one of those methods works and whether it's an efficient method. A method is efficient if it helps you get the job done in a way that is effective (correct) and timely (quick).

Here's an example of an efficient method. You have all gone shopping for groceries with your parents. There are efficient ways to shop for groceries and inefficient ways. When you shop efficiently, you get the job done as quickly as possible without forgetting anything that you need. Here are my steps to an efficient shopping trip: 1) Make a list ahead of time written in the order that my store is arranged; 2) Go to the sections of the store where the items on my list are found and, without looking anywhere else, grab the items I need; and 3) As soon as I have the items on my list, leave the store. Now, this method is only efficient if I always shop at the same store. When I leave one store and go to another, I have to make up a completely different method. The point of our lesson today is not to develop a method that will help your mother shop more efficiently. Our goal today and tomorrow is to figure out how efficient our three processes for multiplication are.

The teacher has developed two different activities to engage students with the three methods. On the first day, she divides the class into three groups. Each group receives one multiplication problem (a 2-digit number times a 2-digit number). The students are directed to prepare a poster advertising the advantages of their particular method along with their version of the problem worked on the poster. When the posters are complete, a spokesperson is chosen to make the case for using the method the group has been assigned along with an explanation of how the students know the answer is correct.

On the second day, each student receives a worksheet divided into three parts. The teacher writes a 2-digit by 2-digit multiplication problem on the board, and she indicates that she wants students to use one of the three methods of multiplication, showing all work in the appropriate box. She gives students three minutes to complete their problem. She tallies how many students chose each method. Then she puts a T-chart up on the SMART Board, and students volunteer the efficiencies and inefficiencies of the three methods. She also queries students about how having more than one method has helped them better understand the multiplication. Their homework for the day consists of completing the assigned multiplication problem using the two methods they didn't choose.

Elementary Nonexample of Examining the Efficiency of Multiple Methods

The nonexample elementary teacher has the same general plan as the example teacher: teach students how to use three different methods for multiplication. However, she leaves it at that point and does not expect the students to peel back the layers of each method and examine the efficiency of each method, and speak and write about those efficiencies.

Secondary Example of Examining Efficiencies of Multiple Methods

The secondary example and nonexample of examining the efficiency of multiple methods take place in an eighth-grade mathematics class. The teacher is working toward the following learning target: Formulating and reasoning about expressions and equations, including modeling an association in bivariate data with a linear equation (see also CCSS Mathematics, Grade 8–Statistics and Probability, Standard 3).

The teacher has experimented during his teaching career with two different methods for teaching students how to solve linear equations. He is not certain about the efficiencies of one method over the other and decides to set up a miniexperiment in his first- and second-period eighth-grade classes. He uses the first method for teaching the multiple methods of solving linear equations in a sequential fashion, teaching one method on day one, and then teaching the second method the next day.

In his second-period class, the teacher uses the compare/contrast approach. He pairs the students and gives each pair a copy of two worked examples showing the two methods. The teacher directs students to take turns describing one of the solutions to their partner. After this discussion, students are directed to answer some accompanying questions that ask them to judge the methods and evaluate their efficiency in solving problems. The teacher finds that his second approach is more effective in the implementation of this technique based on the result he wanted to see in his students (Rittle-Johnson & Star, 2007).

Secondary Nonexample of Examining
Efficiencies and Multiple Methods

The nonexample teacher was working toward the same learning target in terms of students learning multiple ways to solve linear equations, but he did not expect students to engage in discussions of procedural knowledge with classmates or evaluate multiple solutions for their efficiencies.

Determining If Students Can Examine the Efficiencies of Multiple Methods of Problem Solving

Always take time to intentionally monitor whether students have an accurate understanding of various problem-solving methods and are able to evaluate them for their efficiency in obtaining the appropriate solution. To find out who knows and how well they know it, put together a toolkit of assessment approaches. Here are some ways you can monitor your students' understanding of the process of evaluating the efficiency of multiple methods of problem solving:

- Students write explanations of their thinking in their learning logs that the teacher collects and reads.

- Students team up to work problems on the SMART Board while the teacher takes notes on the efficiency and accuracy of their problem solving.

- Students discuss their explanations and justifications while the teacher looks over their shoulders and listens in.

- Students work problems individually on whiteboards that they hold up for the teacher to view.

Use the following student proficiency scale to determine the progress of your students toward examining the efficiencies of multiple methods of problem solving.

Table 3.1: Student Proficiency Scale for Examining Efficiencies and Multiple Methods

Emerging	Fundamental	Desired Result
Students can identify how they solved a problem but cannot explain the rationale for how they arrived at the response or how they would approach a similar problem.	Students can identify how they solved a problem and can offer a limited explanation of the rationale for how they arrived at the response.	Students can identify how they solved a problem, explain why their method was most efficient, and describe how they would approach a similar problem.

Scaffold and Extend Instruction to Meet Students' Needs

There will be students who do not grasp the concept of multiple strategies for solving problems and are not ready for explaining the efficiencies of the various strategies. However, there will be others who are ready to race ahead. Scaffolding and extending for this strategy requires a measure of flexibility combined with two measures of creativity.

Scaffolding

- Directly instruct students on how to use one method at a time. Rather than working on notebook paper, provide students with an organizer containing the appropriate number of labeled boxes to help them keep track of their computations.

- Develop a set of graphic organizers or think sheets on which students can record their thinking.

- Design handouts so that all of the information students need is on one page.

- Pass out only one handout at a time.

- Give only one direction at a time.

Extending

- Students redesign the teacher's graphic organizers for this technique.

- Students develop a YouTube presentation demonstrating both methods of examining efficiencies discussed in this technique.

PART II

SUPPORTING CLAIMS AND ASSERTIONS WITH EVIDENCE

There are three instructional techniques in Part II that will help you show students how to state and support a claim: 1) producing and defending claims from content; 2) identifying and analyzing claims in an author's work; and 3) judging reasoning and evidence in an author's work.

Instructional Technique 4

PRODUCING AND DEFENDING CLAIMS RELATED TO CONTENT

Instructional Technique 4 will help you show your students how to produce and defend claims related to your specific content area. For example, if you teach economics, your students will be expected to produce and defend claims relevant to the specific discipline of economics. Understanding the structure, research methods, and reasoning tools used by the discipline is a powerful way for students to engage with content on a much deeper level. This statement applies to other disciplines as well.

Teaching this technique will initially take more time and mean more work for both you and your students. It requires far more cognitive engagement from students than reading a chapter and taking sketchy notes. However, the time to acquire and practice this skill is worth your investment because the knowledge that students gain will be deeper and longer lasting.

The specialized terms that are essential to mastering this skill are 1) *content*, 2) *claim*, 3) *assertion*, 4) *support*, 5) *grounds*, 6) *backing*, and 7) *qualifiers*. These terms can best be understood by viewing them as part of the following graphic organizer developed for science content. When you use this organizer to introduce the terms to your students, replace the specific content examples with those from you own content area.

Table 4.1: Vocabulary for Producing and Defending Claims

Term	Definition	Example
Content	Textbooks and instructional materials based on content standards	An environmental science textbook, videos, charts, and maps
Claim (sometimes referred to as a thesis or argument)	An idea to be proved	Humans cause global warming.
Assertion	A statement that contains the idea to be proved	Human activity is a substantial cause of global climate change.
Support	Information that is in agreement with and proves the claim. This information can be in the form of grounds and backing.	Human greenhouse gas emissions are causing global climate change.
Grounds	The initial support used to draw the conclusion that becomes the claim	Global warming is evidenced by an increase in the frequency and intensity of tropical cyclones.
Backing	A more developed form of the evidence	From 1975 to 1989, there were 171 category 4 and 5 hurricanes. From 1990 to 2004, there were 269 category 4 and 5 hurricanes.
Qualifiers	Nonexamples or statements that contradict the claim or disprove it	Climate cooling and warming occur in cycles caused by deep ocean currents. These cycles can be shown to coincide with naturally occurring changes in atmospheric and oceanic circulation patterns.

Examples adapted from ProCon.org (2014).

Be aware that your state standards, curricular and assessment materials, and the CCSS may use different terms—albeit with similar definitions—to those found in the organizer. For example, CCR Anchor Standard, Reading, Standard #8 states, "Delineate and evaluate the argument and specific claims in a text, including the validity of the reasoning as well as the relevance and sufficiency of the evidence." (Common Core State Standards Initiative, 2010a)

The first step to effectively implementing this technique is to agree on a common language that aligns with the standards, curricula, and assessments of a specific grade level or department. School-wide alignment is preferable, but departmental alignment is essential. The Grades 6–8 Writing Standards for ELA and literacy in history/social studies, science, and technical subjects state that students in Grades 6–8 should be able to write arguments focused on discipline-specific content using the following steps:

1. Introduce claim(s) about a topic or issue, acknowledge and distinguish the claim(s) from alternate or opposing claims, and organize the reasons and evidence logically.

2. Support claim(s) with logical reasoning and relevant, accurate data and evidence that demonstrate an understanding of the topic or text, using credible sources.

3. Use words, phrases, and clauses to create cohesion and clarify the relationships among claim(s), counterclaims, reasons, and evidence.

4. Establish and maintain a formal style.

5. Provide a concluding statement or section that follows from and supports the argument presented.

How to Effectively Implement Producing and Defending Claims from Content

The effective implementation of producing and defending claims from content is a two-part process. Students must first process the text. As defined in CCR Anchor Standard for Reading 1, processing involves reading closely to determine what the text says explicitly and making logical inferences from it. In addition, the process involves citing specific textual evidence when writing or speaking to support conclusions drawn from the text. Jumping into the deep end by attempting to implement producing and defending claims from content without first having extracted meaning from the text is a waste of time. Meaningful learning begins with reading and understanding text and then using what has been read to develop an organized and coherent body of information. The following table illustrates the steps involved in processing the text. After processing content, students will be ready to produce and defend claims from the content. Select content text that is written on an easier reading level. This will free up your students' working memories to pay attention to the steps needed to produce and defend claims from content. Also, select content text with an obvious claim and enough key details that show support of the claim. The text you select for the initial introduction to students can make the difference between success and failure.

Table 4.2: Steps in a Lesson for Processing Content

Step	Discussion
1. Select the content-related, standards-aligned text you plan to use.	You may wish to use content text written at an easier reading level during your initial instruction.
2. Identify the text structure (the way the author has organized the text).	There is an assumption at this point that you will have taught various types of text structure or at least the type of structure you are providing to your students for reading. To scaffold this exercise for students, give them clues to help them understand the structure. For example, if the author makes comparisons and points out contrasts in order to explain, make information clear, show evidence of something, or make a case for something, the structure is comparison/contrast. Other text structures that are good choices for showing students how to examine and analyze the strength of support presented in content are cause/effect and problem/solution.
3. Select an organizer that is appropriate for the text structure you have selected and model for students how to complete the organizer on a small chunk of text.	If you are new to the process of thinking aloud for students about the decisions you make as you complete the organizer, rehearse it ahead of time. The rehearsal process will reveal any glitches and prevent them from derailing your lesson.
4. Chunk the text into manageable units and have students identify the elements of the text structure chunk by chunk as they complete their organizers.	If your class has a majority of struggling students, you may wish to scaffold their completion of the text by using a helper to work with you in your demonstration.

After students have processed the text (extracted meaning from it and determined the central idea or themes), they will be prepared to dig deeper into the content to produce and defend a claim they discovered during their reading. The following discussion fleshes out how to walk students through the initial instruction of Instructional Technique 4. Give students a copy of the organizer shown at the introduction to the technique and remind them of the specifics of each of the various categories: claim, grounds, backing, and qualifiers.

Although you may have expected students to process and derive meaning from the content text independently, you will want to provide some assistance to them as they produce and defend a claim based on what they earlier read in the content text.

1. *Assist students with identifying a claim from their initial interactions with the content.*

First, review with students the information they extracted in their initial exposure to the content. Lead them to identify the central idea from the notes they took on the organizer you provided to scaffold their first reading of the text. That central idea will likely be a good candidate for a claim. The claim can also be framed as a conclusion based on all that students have learned about the topic to include previous knowledge and experiences that might inform the new content.

2. *Help students define the initial support (i.e., identify the grounds for the claim).*

To help students establish grounds, prompt them to cite the central idea that caused them to believe that the claim they produced is appropriate. Avoid thinking for students whenever possible. You might provide struggling students with the claim and then ask them to identify why it may or may not be true. The students would still be expected to articulate reasons for the claim, state an expert opinion, cite experimental evidence, and quote factual information as well as share an explanation of common knowledge as they develop the grounds for that claim.

3. *Have students develop backing (additional support) for the claim.*

In this step, the teacher leads students to further explore the body of information that is available to them regarding their claim. Support students in this phase by helping them to identify the appropriate resources to identify support for the assertion.

4. *Have students frame the qualifier (exceptions or counterarguments to the claim).*

In this final step, lead students to sources that may provide alternative points of view to the claim. Well-written texts often provide qualifiers as part of the content presentation.

The following organizer provides a framework for students to record the information they identified from their reading. It prompts them with questions to answer, leading them from step to step. Taking notes on an organizer such as this helps to solidify key concepts and enable students to generate solid long-term memory about critical content. Depending on your students and their expertise, consider using this organizer to model how you would go about producing and defending a claim. Think aloud for students about the decision-making process as you go through it to produce and defend a claim from content.

Table 4.3: How to Produce and Defend a Claim From Content

How to Think	Question to Answer	Action to Take
Identify the claim: a conclusion you have reached from your reading, an idea that needs to be proved.	What is the central idea that the content suggests to you?	Write the claim here.
Identify the grounds: essential evidence and reasoning for the claim.	What are some key details that give initial support to the claim?	Write the details here.
Identify the backing: additional support for the groups.	What types of expert opinion, experimental evidence, or factual information add further support to the claim?	List the additional types of support here.
Frame the qualifiers: exceptions to the claim, often expressed as the counterargument.	What types of information serve as nonexamples of the claim? Can you "disprove" any of the claims or offer alternative points of view?	List the qualifiers here.

Common Mistakes

There are many ways you can lose or confuse students when implementing this technique:

- The teacher omits the process of directly instructing students in how to extract meaning from the text.

- The teacher uses content text that is too difficult for many of the students.

- The teacher uses content text that does not have an obvious structure so that students can readily identify a claim and supporting details.

- The teacher does not adequately model by thinking aloud so that students can see how a skilled thinker tackles an assignment like this.

- The teacher tells students what to write down in each of the boxes in the organizer and does not hold them responsible for thinking.

- The teacher does more telling than prompting and facilitating.

- The teacher does not give students adequate time to process and understand the content before asking them to manipulate it at a higher level by producing and defending a claim.

- The teacher does not insist on clearly stated support for the claims that students make.

- The teacher accepts insufficient backing and unrelated evidence, thereby encouraging careless thinking and lack of accountability on the part of students.

- The teacher accepts faulty logic in the interest of not embarrassing students or being too eager to cover the material and move on.

Examples and Nonexamples of Producing and Defending Claims Related to Content

Following are two examples (one elementary and one secondary) and their corresponding nonexamples of producing and defending claims. As you read, think about experiences you have had in your classroom. Consider the common mistakes and note how the example teachers cleverly avoid them and the nonexample teachers miss the mark by making one of these common mistakes.

*Elementary Example of Producing and Defending Claims
Related to Content*

The elementary example and nonexample illustrate producing and defending claims related to content. The example teacher is focused on both a content standard and a reading standard. The content standard is "Describe the expedition of Lewis and Clark from 1803 to 1806." (*Massachusetts History and Social Science Curriculum Framework*, Grade 5)

The reading standard states that students will be able to "explain how an author uses reasons and evidence to support particular points in a text, identifying which reasons and evidence support which points" (CCSS ELA & Literacy, Reading–Informational Text Grade 5, Standard #8).

In the following example, the teacher explains for students what will transpire in the lesson he has designed.

> Class, today we are going to learn how to produce and defend a claim. Those are fancy words. To produce means to make something, and a claim is something that you think is true about what you read. To defend a claim, you need to give some proof that the claim is true. Now, watch me as I produce and defend a claim. Here's my claim: This class is one of the best classes that I have ever taught. Now, I have to defend that claim. *The teacher writes two statements on the SMART Board: 1) This class has fewer disciplinary referrals than any class I have ever taught. 2) This class has more honor roll students than any class I have ever taught.* See what I mean? Now, I just made up that claim and evidence, although you are a wonderful class. If I were going to support my claim, I would have to get out all of my class records for all of my fifteen years of teaching. I could do it, if I had to. Now, the claims that you will produce and the evidence you find to defend your claims will come from our social studies book. We've been reading about the Lewis and Clark expedition, and you already know a great deal about it.

After this brief introduction, the teacher goes on to think aloud about one section of the text, producing two claims: 1) Thomas Jefferson's imagination led to the exploration and settlement of the West; and 2) Lewis and Clark's courage and determination led to the exploration and settlement of the West. He asks students to get together with their partner, choose one of the claims, and fill out their organizer with grounds and backing to support the chosen claim. The content text does not contain enough information for students to frame qualifiers. However, the teacher plans to have them work with several primary sources and other resources later to identify any counterclaims or qualifiers to fully flesh out their thinking about the content.

The teacher planned well. His students had already processed the content text before he asked them to defend two claims. He provided an example of the terms drawn from real life. He modeled producing the claim to scaffold the process. However, students were expected to independently identify grounds and backing in the content text. He gave them further opportunities to solidify their content knowledge by expecting them to find qualifiers in more diverse instructional materials.

Elementary Nonexample of Producing and Defending Claims Related to Content

The following elementary nonexample is based on the same grade level and standards. The teacher decided that time constraints prohibited him from processing the content one day and learning how to produce and defend claims on a second day. So, he designed one long lesson. That was his first mistake. Students got bogged down in the content because the teacher didn't allocate enough time. Then, when he transitioned to teaching the technique, he hurriedly defined the terms but did not provide an example to help students understand the terms. He had neglected to choose claims ahead of time, having not really rehearsed his think-aloud. The teacher was confused, and so were his students. He decided at the last minute to assign the entire process to the students to see who could do it and who could not. He discovered that very few of his students grasped either the content or the process.

Secondary Example of Producing and Defending Claims

The following secondary example is based on producing and defending claims in a class on US history. The teacher is working toward two learning targets:

- Analyze Abraham Lincoln's presidency, the Emancipation Proclamation (1863), his views on slavery, and the political obstacles he encountered. (*Massachusetts History and Social Science Curriculum Framework,* Grades 7–12).

- Cite strong and thorough textual evidence to support analysis of what the text says explicitly as well as inferences drawn from the text, including determining where the text leaves matters uncertain. (CCSS ELA & Literacy, Reading Grades 11–12, Standard #1).

Our example teacher has carefully examined his textbook's unit on the Civil War. With each section of the unit, he has developed activities to ensure his students are explicitly gaining meaning from the text. However, he plans to teach his students how to produce and defend claims about the content because there are many opportunities to do so during the course of the unit. He has designed an organizer to be used throughout the unit. The first section of text is focused on the antecedents of the Civil War suggesting claim(s) about the causes of the war. The second claim might hypothesize the turning point or climax. The third claim could well be about the most significant outcomes of the war.

> Class, you've been doing some outstanding reasoning and writing throughout our Civil War unit. Judging from the quality of the writing in your learning logs and the kinds of discussion I'm hearing in your small groups, I've decided you are ready for a new challenge. When you master the technique I'll be teaching you today, you will be well prepared for the state assessment when it turns up in April. The technique is called producing and defending claims. There are lots of different careers that use this technique on a daily basis: Lawyers, judges, law enforcement officers, and members of the FBI and the CIA all have to produce and defend claims every day. Even the president of the United States has to do this to convince Congress or the American people of the worthiness of a claim he is making.

Our claims and evidence must all relate to the Civil War content that we have covered during the past couple of weeks. I am passing out a handout that contains the key terms you'll need to know. Keep it handy since you'll be using it every day this week. I guarantee that by the end of the week, you will understand the Civil War well enough to write a five-page report on it. But, I'm not going to assign one unless there are some eager beavers looking for extra credit to wipe out those failed quiz grades.

To get his students started, he hands out a copy of the organizer titled "How to Produce and Defend a Claim from Content." Students will complete one of these organizers for each of the sections of the textbook's unit on the Civil War. To get them started, the teacher thinks aloud about how he has been able to produce a claim. He has parts of the text showing on the SMART Board and underlines and circles various words and statements that have helped him develop his claim. He wants to demonstrate to his students that producing the claim takes thinking and rereading the text even though they have already read it once. This technique often requires digging deeper than most students do during their first reading of a text. Once the teacher has modeled producing his claim, he asks if there is a volunteer who would like to think along with him to identify some key details that will form the initial support for the claim. This initial support, he reminds them, is called the grounds. He now asks for another volunteer to help him identify the backing, further evidence to support the claim. The assignment for today is to find a different claim that could be made from the text the teacher was using for a model. This is a good exercise for students who think that reading something once is enough.

Secondary Nonexample of Producing and Defending Claims

The nonexample teacher is working from the same content and reading standards as the example teacher. She does not feel comfortable modeling her reasoning aloud and believes that thinking aloud will be too babyish for her students and too embarrassing for her. She has already decided that spending any more time on the Civil War unit is time she does not have. She therefore decides to complete the organizer for the first section on her own and hand it out to her students as a model to follow for their homework assignment: Use this same method to produce and defend a claim using the written model. The teacher does not realize the power of first modeling for students, then working with a student volunteer, and then finally having students work as partners. All of these steps are the preamble to students producing and defending claims independently. The majority of the students in this class failed to complete the assignment correctly.

Determining If Students Can Produce and Defend a Claim From Content

Monitoring is an integral part of the instructional process and should always have two components: 1) something that students do to demonstrate the desired result of the technique (in this instance produce and defend a claim related to content); and 2) something that the teacher does to check for the desired result and respond to students' progress. Here are some specific examples that apply to producing and defending claims:

- Students complete an organizer showing their understanding of content text and their ability to produce and defend a claim related to specific content.

- Students can orally state a claim they have produced and describe the central idea of the content from which the claim is derived.

- Students can defend their claim orally with at least two descriptions of evidence from the content.

The following student proficiency scale will help you assess how your students are progressing in their abilities to produce and defend a claim related to content. Use the scale to refine the precise ways you plan to identify the results of your instruction.

Table 4.4: Student Proficiency Scale for Producing and Defending a Claim Related to Content

Emerging	Fundamental	Desired Result
Students can define the terms—*claim*, *grounds*, *backing*, and *qualifier*—but cannot apply them in their own reading, reasoning, and writing.	Students can state a claim of their own related to the content, but can offer only limited support, minimal backing, and few qualifiers if any.	Students can successfully state a claim of their own related to the content, establish grounds, and provide backing and frame qualifiers.

Scaffold and Extend Instruction to Meet Students' Needs

There will likely be one or more students who do not grasp precisely how to produce and defend a claim the first time the process is explained to them. Similarly, there are students who "got it" and "had it" seemingly before you even "taught it." Meeting the needs of these two diverse groups of students requires that you adapt your instruction. The more focused you are on designing instruction for all students, the more ground you will gain with students on either end of the achievement continuum. Here are some ideas for developing scaffolding and extending to meet students' needs.

Scaffolding

- Use content texts at easier reading levels to scaffold the process part of extracting explicit meaning from the text.

- Provide ample amounts of modeling so students can hear the thinking aloud of a student who gets it.

- Give struggling students the claim statement and expect them to identify the grounds and the backing.

Extending

- Provide an individual or a small group with a more advanced claim from the content than could be inferred from the textbook. Have the individual or group of students develop supporting evidence from sources they locate digitally.

- Ask an individual or small group to provide alternative claims from the text and find support for them in other sources.

Instructional Technique 5

IDENTIFYING AND ANALYZING CLAIMS IN AN AUTHOR'S WORK

This instructional technique is based on the key terms and thinking described in Instructional Technique 4 with one difference. Using that technique, you taught students how to produce and defend claims based on their reading and understanding of critical content.

Instructional Technique 5 requires a change of perspective on the part of the learner. Students are expected to read text written by named authors and produce claims and supporting evidence from the text about the author's relationship to the topic, the text structure the author uses, the author's attitude or posture toward the subject, and the author's purpose for writing. Content produced by named authors includes books—fiction and nonfiction—as well as articles in journals, opinion pieces in newspapers, and blogs by named authors on the Internet.

Content textbooks, particularly those at the K–12 level, are written by multiple authors. This author team or committee seeks to be as invisible as possible, striving for a straightforward style that does not distract from the critical content. On the other hand, authors whose names appear on the cover of a book have a specific purpose for writing as well as a unique style. They have a story to tell, a subject to share. While reading their works, students can identify the claims they make as well as analyze how these claims are impacted by the author's purpose and style.

How to Effectively Implement Identifying and Analyzing Claims in an Author's Work

The following tables will lead you through the steps of identifying and analyzing claims in an author's work: 1) "Vocabulary for Producing and Defending Claims" (see Table 4.1 in Instructional Technique 4); 2) "Key Terms for Identifying and Analyzing Claims in an Author's Work" in Table 5.1; and 3) "How to Identify and Analyze Claims in an Author's Work" following the key terms.

If you have not yet implemented Instructional Technique 4 with your students, read through Table 4.1 "Vocabulary for Producing and Defending Claims" in the previous section. The key concepts in that table must be mastered in order to implement this technique. Additionally, there are several other key terms that are applicable only to this strategy. They are defined in the following table.

Table 5.1: Key Terms for Identifying and Analyzing Claims in an Author's Work

Term	Definition
Purpose	The reason for which an author writes a book or article
Text Structure	The way an author decides to organize a book or article
Style	How an author uses language

The following organizer can be used in two ways: 1) as a template on which to plan your think-aloud for students about how you identify and analyze claims in an author's work, and 2) as an organizer for students to complete as they work together or individually to identify and analyze claims in an author's work.

Table 5.2: How to Identify and Analyze Claims in an Author's Work

What to do	Question	Write your answers to the questions
Identify the claim: a conclusion you have reached about what the author believes from your reading	What is the central idea that the content suggests to you?	Write the central idea/ claim here.

(continued on next page)

Table 5.2 (continued)

What to do	Question	Write your answers to the questions
Identify the grounds: essential evidence and reasoning that the author provides to support the claim.	What are some key details that give initial support to the claim?	Write the details here.
Identify the backing: any additional support that the author provides.	What types of expert opinion, experimental evidence, or factual information add further support to the claim?	List the additional types of support here.
Frame the qualifiers: exceptions to the claim, often expressed as the counterargument.	What types of information serve as nonexamples of the claim? Can you "disprove" any of the claims or offer alternative points of view?	List the qualifiers here.
Describe the author's purpose for writing the book or article.	What is the author's point of view?	Describe how you identified the author's point of view.
Describe the text structure the author uses.	What type of text structure does the author use? Some examples include pointing out similarities and differences, sharing many anecdotes and stories, and using a great deal of statistics and data.	Describe how you identified the author's text structure.
Describe the author's style.	What are some key features of this author's style?	Describe how you identified the author's style.

Common Mistakes

The most common mistakes to avoid when implementing identifying and analyzing claims in an author's work include the following:

- The teacher does not gain complete mastery of the various key terms before implementing the technique.

- The teacher chooses text that is too difficult or does not contain clear examples of the various aspects of an author's approach to writing: purpose, structure, and style.

- The teacher does not adequately model and think aloud for students how to identify and analyze claims in an author's work.

- The teacher does not hold students accountable for engaging in the higher-level thinking skills required in this technique.

- The teacher does not allocate sufficient time for directly instructing students in the meanings of key terms.

- The teacher does not provide sufficient examples for students.

Examples and Nonexamples of Identifying and Analyzing Claims in an Author's Work

The following examples and nonexamples demonstrate identifying and analyzing claims in an author's work.

Elementary Example of Identifying and Analyzing Claims in an Author's Work

The example classroom is a fourth-grade language arts class. The teacher is addressing three learning targets:

- Determine the main idea of a text and explain how it is supported by key details; summarize the text.

- Describe the overall structure (e.g., chronology, comparison, cause/effect, problem/solution) of events, ideas, concepts, or information in a text or part of a text.

- Explain how an author uses reasons and evidence to support particular points in a text (CCSS ELA & Literacy, Reading–Informational Text, Grade 4, Standards #2, 5, 8).

The teacher has been working since the beginning of the school year on helping his students determine the main ideas and writing summaries of the text. It is the second semester, and he is pleased with the way his students are progressing. He now allocates two weeks to teaching his fourth graders how to identify various types of text structure. Once again, with very few exceptions his students are gaining proficiency every day.

He hopes that the lesson today will build on the solid skills they have acquired thus far and help them add one more way to read and comprehend text: figuring out how authors use reason and evidence to support particular points in the text. He plans to adapt this technique to his fourth graders and decides to use the language of the CCSS standard. Students' abilities to identify main idea and details along with their growing knowledge about text structures will enable them to do a credible job of implementing this technique. The secret to his success as he implements the technique is his choice of text. It is easy to read so all of his students will be able to extract meaning from it. Further, it contains several claims about climate change and global warming—topics his students hear about frequently on the news or see on the Internet. They have brought several articles for current events on the topic.

A prominent community member has written an opinion piece for the local newspaper. It contains several claims, thereby giving the teacher an opportunity to think aloud for his students about how he identifies and analyzes a claim this author has made. Here's how he introduces his lesson:

> Good morning, everybody. Are you ready to do some serious thinking? We're going to be thinking about two related subjects that a lot of people are talking about, especially since we all experienced that big hurricane last year: global warming and climate change. We are going to use two big thinking skills we have been working on for a long time: determining the main idea and details about something we read and then figuring out what kind of text structure the author used to tell us about the main idea and details. Remember, if you need a reminder about what those words mean, you can check out the vocabulary chart at the back of the room. Or, you can use the copy in your language arts notebook. I'm going to add one new word to our chart today: *claim*. A claim is an idea to be proved. We are going to look for claims in the article we're going to read. See if we can figure out what main idea the author wants to prove to us, and then we're going to look for evidence that proves it. Evidence, you remember, is something authors write that proves that the claim they stated is accurate.

This lesson will stretch over at least two days. The teacher will think aloud about finding the first claim and the evidence to support it. Students will read the same section once again to identify the text structure. The teacher gives them three possible choices: problem/solution, cause/effect, and compare/contrast. In the follow-up lesson, students will assume the responsibility for working with their partners to identify the second claim and its supporting evidence.

Elementary Nonexample

The nonexample teacher has high hopes and big dreams but fails to choose that just-right text to model how she identifies and analyzes claims in an author's work. She realizes too late that she has not carefully thought through each step of the lesson in advance. She did not have clear learning targets that were grade-level appropriate, and her lesson lacked focus. Students were frustrated and inattentive.

Secondary Example of Identifying and Analyzing Claims in an Author's Work

The example is from a ninth-grade English class where students are reading an informational text. The teacher is working toward three learning targets:

- Cite strong and thorough textual evidence to support analysis of what the text says explicitly as well as inferences drawn from the text.

- Analyze in detail how an author's ideas or claims are developed.

- Determine an author's point of view or purpose in a text and analyze how an author uses rhetoric to advance that point of view or purpose (CCSS ELA & Literacy, Reading–Informational Text Grades 9–10, Standards #1, 5, 6).

The teacher has selected two different opinion articles dealing with the topic of climate change. He will model the technique from one of the articles and assign the second article to his students to identify and analyze the claims. Eventually the students will reanalyze both of the articles to write a compare/contrast essay.

However, at the outset of this lesson, the teacher is directly teaching the new terms that are unfamiliar to students. He has often been puzzled about the most effective way to teach students the vast amount of new vocabulary. He recently watched a video of a teacher using a choral response method to teach students how to pronounce, spell, and define new terms. He was impressed with how little time this method took and how engaged all of the students seemed to be. Since that experience, he has routinely taught new academic vocabulary using the method. The key to the success of this method is the short student-friendly definitions he provides for the vocabulary. The pithy definitions are easier for students to use in a choral response. He always teaches and reviews new vocabulary the minute the bell rings. The exercise settles and engages students immediately.

Good morning, everyone. Are you ready to learn some new terms? Here we go.

Directly Instructing Students in New Academic Vocabulary

Teacher: Word 1 is **claim**. What word? *Gives signal by dropping hand or snapping fingers.*

Students: **Claim**.

Teacher: A claim is an idea to be proved. What is the meaning of **claim**? *Gives signal.*

Students: An idea to be proved.

Teacher: In our work today, we will be identifying a claim in an article written by an author.

Teacher: Word 2 is **evidence**. What word? *Gives signal.*

Students: **Evidence**.

Teacher: Evidence is textual proof that supports a claim. What is the meaning of **evidence**? *Gives signal.*

Students: Textual proof that supports a claim.

Teacher: In our work today, we are going to look for evidence in the written words in the book to prove the claim we identified.

Teacher: Word 3 is **grounds**. What word? *Gives signal.*

Students: **Grounds**.

Teacher: Grounds are the initial support for a claim. What is the meaning of **grounds**? *Gives signal.*

Students: Initial support for a claim.

Teacher: Word 4 is **backing**. What word? *Gives signal.*

Students: **Backing**.

Teacher: Backing is even more support for the claim. What is the meaning of **backing**? *Gives signal.*

Students: Even more support for the claim.

Teacher: In our work today, we are going to identify a claim in an article written by an author and then find evidence in the form of grounds and backing.

Teacher: Word 5 is **qualifiers**. What word? *Gives signal.*

Students: **Qualifiers**.

Teacher: Qualifiers are statements that contradict the claim. What is the meaning of **qualifiers**? *Gives signal.*

Students: Qualifiers are statements that contradict the claim.

Once students have been introduced to and practiced the new vocabulary, the teacher hands out the organizer he will use to model the technique for students. With the time remaining in the class period, students find their partners and begin combing the second text.

Secondary Nonexample of Identifying and
Analyzing Claims in an Author's Work

The nonexample teacher spends little time on directly instructing academic vocabulary. He believes that students should be able to pick it up on the fly. However, his students consistently do poorly on sample tests where they are prompted to write a constructed response that always uses at least five to six academic words. When students do not have these terms firmly secured in their long-term memory, they frequently lose confidence in their ability to engage in the process.

Determining If Students Can Identify and Analyze Claims in an Author's Work

You will only know if your instruction is getting the desired result if your students are demonstrating as many ways as possible that they are conversant with the meanings of the multiple terms and can find examples in the work of any author and summarize them.

Consider the types of actions your students will carry out to demonstrate their mastery, and at the same time, figure out a variety of monitoring actions to listen, look for, read, check, inspect, or otherwise determine that your students are making progress along the monitoring scale.

Here are some suggestions for monitoring your students:

- Collect completed organizers that show work that students have completed independently.

- When students are working in small groups, walk around the room and intentionally watch and listen for students' usage of the terms in appropriate contexts.

- Carefully monitor when you are directly teaching new academic vocabulary. From time to time, ask individual students to respond. You will soon discover who has not mastered the pronunciations and meaning of new academic vocabulary.

Table 5.3: Student Proficiency Scale for Identifying and Analyzing Claims in an Author's Work

Emerging	Fundamental	Desired Result
Students can define the terms *claim, grounds, backing, qualifiers, style, purpose,* and *text structure* but cannot identify these concepts in an author's work.	Students can identify claims, grounds, backing, qualifiers, purpose, text structure, and style in an author's work, but are unable to analyze the claims of the author as they relate to the author's purpose, content, and style.	Students can successfully identify claims, grounds, backing, and qualifiers in an author's work and analyze those claims as they relate to the author's purpose, content, and style.

Scaffold and Extend Instruction to Meet Students' Needs

When you encounter a small group or individual who is having difficulty or, on the other hand, is well beyond your present instructional level, develop some activities to meet their special needs.

Scaffolding

- Provide prompts and sentence starters in the context of the organizer.

- Ask students to practice the directly instructing exercise at home with a sibling or parent.

- When available, use aides or paraprofessionals to preteach some of the aspects of this technique so students have the benefit of prior knowledge.

Extending

- Create rebuttals to the claims of an author.

- Utilize the technique by identifying and analyzing the claims of more challenging works by various authors.

- Have students use this technique by comparing two works by the same author written at different times in the author's career.

- Have students use this technique by comparing the works of two different authors writing on the same topic.

Instructional Technique 6

JUDGING REASONING AND EVIDENCE IN AN AUTHOR'S WORK

The final instructional technique in this guide will help you teach students how to reason at a more advanced level than have previous techniques in this guide. Students are expected not only to identify specific claims and evidence in the work of an author, but also evaluate whether an author's reasoning is valid and whether the evidence the author provides is sufficient and relevant.

These terms are derived from the eighth CCR Anchor Standard for Reading: "Delineate and evaluate the argument and specific claims in a text, including the validity of the reasoning as well as the relevance and sufficiency of the evidence." If you are currently working on the implementation of this specific CCR standard with your students, you already know the challenge it presents. However, just ahead there are some specific steps you can take with your students to guide you to effective implementation. Several terms are unique to the standard and to this technique. They are defined and discussed in the table titled "Key Terms for the Implementation of Instructional Technique 6."

Table 6.1: Key Terms for the Implementation of Instructional Technique 6

Term	Definition	Discussion
Delineate	To identify and explain something in explicit detail	In the context of this technique, students will read the text to identify the author's claim, backing, and qualifiers, and then outline the evidence.
Evaluate	Make up one's mind about the value of something	In the context of this technique, students will decide if the author's reasoning is valid and whether the evidence provided is relevant and sufficient.

(continued on next page)

Table 6.1 (continued)

Term	Definition	Discussion
Defensible	Valid	Reasoning is valid when it doesn't contain any errors, as defined in Instructional Technique 1.
Sufficient	Enough	Evidence is sufficient if the author has provided enough of it to cause the reader to take the claim seriously.
Relevant	Connected	The evidence is relevant if the various pieces of evidence are related to the claim and are also presented in a logical progression, one after another.

How to Effectively Implement Judging Reasoning and Evidence in an Author's Work

Effectively showing students how to judge the validity of author reasoning and further evaluate the worth of the presented evidence can be done only if they have a growing understanding of the concepts and processes covered in the earlier techniques in this guide. Students may not be able to produce definitions or explanations of all of the multiple errors of reasoning on command, but they do need to understand the concept represented in the error and believe that errors in reasoning do exist. At that point they are ready to have in their hands a comprehensive list of those errors to consult as part of this technique.

Students must understand that the things they say during class discussions, and the products they write must be well reasoned (i.e., logical). To return to a phrase from a prior technique, the phrase must make sense. As you well know, these types of skills are not mastered as one would memorize battles of the Civil War or learn the multiplication tables. They will need to be directly taught, constantly modeled, frequently practiced, and always expected. After the process begins, you will soon see growing evidence that students' abilities are progressing.

Table 6.2: Lesson Steps for Judging and Reasoning in an Author's Work

Lesson Step	Discussion
1. Select the standard and content that you intend to be the focus of your lesson.	Always connect the technique to the relevant standard and content.
2. Directly instruct students about the meaning of the new terms found in Table 5.1 "Key Terms for Identifying and Analyzing Claims in an Author's Work."	Use the scripted text on pages 71 and 72 of Instructional Technique 5 as a guide for directly teaching new academic vocabulary.
3. Directly instruct students about the meaning of the examples and nonexamples found in Table 6.3 "Examples and Nonexamples of Reasoning and Evidence."	This set of examples and nonexamples can be used by students as a reference during implementation.
4. Model this technique using text at an easier reading level so students can more readily follow your reasoning about the text. As you model, use Table 6.4 "Judging Reasoning and Evidence in an Author's Work" to evaluate the text in terms of the author's reasoning, as well as the sufficiency and relevance of the evidence.	Remember to prepare and rehearse your modeling well in advance of the class. As you become more skilled at thinking aloud, you can do it at the spur of the moment in the context of a fast-moving class discussion. But in the beginning, prepare ahead.
5. Prepare copies of a blank organizer for students to complete as they begin to implement this technique.	Avoid working through an organizer yourself and having students copy your thinking on their organizer. They might copy your thinking as a sample to consult while they work. However, insist on students doing their own thinking.

Table 6.3: Examples and Nonexamples of Reasoning and Evidence

Defensible Reasoning Examples	Indefensible Reasoning Examples
The reasoning is logical and makes sense. The reasoning supports the claim and the backing.	The reasoning contains one or more of the errors of reasoning described in Instructional Technique 1. These inaccuracies can reduce the truth and validity of a claim. Although the reasoning seems to support the claim, it needs to be qualified to sufficiently and fairly support the claim.

(continued on next page)

Table 6.3 (continued)

Relevant Evidence Examples	Irrelevant Evidence Examples
The evidence directly relates to the claim and the backing. The author uses quotations and citations from experts in the field. The author uses credible and trustworthy sources of information.	The evidence is drawn from fields of study that are only tangentially related to the claim. The evidence is drawn from many unrelated fields, and the author fails to connect the evidence.
Sufficient Evidence Examples	Insufficient Evidence Examples
The author supports the claim from a variety of sources of information. The author uses a variety of types of evidence to include facts and statistical data.	The evidence to support the claim comes from a single source. The evidence relies too heavily on the opinion and expertise of the author. Quotations from experts are not skillfully woven in the line of reasoning.

Table 6.4: Judging Reasoning and Evidence in an Author's Work

Ask the Question	Circle Yes or No	Explain Your Decision
Is the author's claim valid?	Yes or No	
Is the author's evidence relevant?	Yes or No	
Is the author's evidence sufficient?	Yes or No	

Common Mistakes

Common mistakes in this instructional technique are similar to those identified in other techniques related to students producing and supporting claims in Instructional Techniques 4 and 5. Here are some additional mistakes to watch for:

- The teacher doesn't plan for modeling and thinking aloud in advance of teaching the technique.

- The teacher uses a book that is too difficult for students to read and understand while at the same time learning a new thinking skill.

- The teacher does not develop enough examples to enable students to clearly distinguish between valid/indefensible, relevant/irrelevant, and sufficient/insufficient.

- The teacher does not provide wait time for students to process difficult text.

- The teacher does not give students enough opportunities to learn new vocabulary.

Examples and Nonexamples of Judging Reasoning and Evidence in the Classroom

Following are two examples (one elementary and one secondary) and their corresponding nonexamples of judging reasoning. Consider the common mistakes, and note how the example teachers plan ahead to avoid them and the nonexample teachers miss the mark by making one or more of these common mistakes.

Elementary Example of Judging Reasoning and Evidence

The first example and nonexample illustrate judging reasoning and evidence at the elementary level. The learning target states, "Explain how an author uses reasons and evidence to support particular points in a text, identifying which reasons and evidence support which points." (CCSS ELA & Literacy, Reading–Informational Text Grade 5, Standard #8)

The teacher of this fifth-grade class has known for some time that she plans to teach her students how to judge reasoning and evidence in the work of an author. To that end, she has been collecting examples of short articles appearing in the Op-Ed section of her newspaper. She has watched for articles written by named individuals, especially individuals who have expertise in a field they are writing about. In the example, the teacher begins by explaining to her students the purpose of the day's lesson. She has often been able to find articles that represent very different points of view on the same subject. One such set of articles deals with the dangers of smoking. Finding opinion articles on the reading level of her students is a challenge, but she believes these two articles are perfect. There is one for her to read and model for students and a second one for them to work on partially with partners. Individual students will be responsible for completing the organizer independently.

Before her students arrive to class, the teacher sets up her overhead projector with a copy of the text from which she is going to think aloud. She projects a copy of her organizer up on the SMART Board. This setup allows her to move back and forth between the text and the organizer.

> Good morning, class. We've been talking about the dangers of smoking in our health class, and I found two articles in the newspaper written by different authors that we are going to analyze. To analyze means to take something apart and look at it very closely. These authors make some very strong claims or ideas that they want to prove to us, the readers. Our job is to pick apart what they have written to figure out if their claims are valid and we can trust what they say. In order to do that, we have to look for evidence in the words they have written. We want to find out if there's enough evidence to convince us that their claim is valid or trustworthy, and we also need to decide whether there's enough evidence and the evidence makes sense to us.

Once the teacher has identified a claim in the text, she writes it on her organizer. She explains that now that she has identified the claim, she needs to look for evidence. She reads aloud another short section of the text and asks students to talk with a partner to see if they can point out any good evidence to support the author's claim. One pair of partners volunteer, and they come to the front to put the number 1 beside the first piece of evidence. The teacher works through the rest of the article one chunk at a time, urging her students to think about and figure out with a partner where the evidence is. Almost all students have at least one chance to come to the front and mark a piece of evidence.

The teacher writes this evidence on her organizer that she has simplified for her younger students. Now, they are going to decide if there is enough good evidence in the article to support the claim. They do this by answering the question in the organizer titled "Judging Reasoning and Evidence in an Author's Work."

Elementary Nonexample of Judging Reasoning and Evidence

The nonexample teacher skips over any introduction of terms and setting of the stage. She does not model and think aloud for students. She simply hands out copies of the article and organizer and directs students to complete the assignment in their groups of four. She is unaware that two of the groups have encountered difficulties and are talking about an upcoming event at school over the weekend. Her mistakes are many. They could have been avoided by preplanning, providing an anticipatory set for the lesson, preparing and rehearsing a think-aloud, and carefully monitoring what her students were doing. You could identify other mistakes as well.

Secondary Example of Judging Reasoning and Evidence

The secondary example and nonexample come from an eighth-grade language arts classroom and are based the following learning target: Delineate and evaluate the argument and specific claims in a text, assessing whether the reasoning is sound and the evidence is relevant and sufficient; identify false statements and fallacious reasoning. (CCSS ELA & Literacy, Reading–Informational Text Grades 9–10, Standard #8) Here's how she introduces the assignment to students.

> Class, you have been working very diligently this semester on a very difficult learning standard. *The teacher has written out the above standard on the board.* I want to remind you of some of the new terms we've learned. *The teacher points to a chart on the wall containing the important terms and their meanings.* In a few short weeks, you will be taking an assessment to measure how well you have mastered this standard. Some of you may feel very confident, but others are still a little shaky. I am going to model for you exactly how I would tackle an assignment like this using an article about global warming. Listen as I tell you what's going through my mind while I read this article and decide how to answer the questions in the organizer.

The teacher has duplicated an article about global warming for students to read. She incorporates many of the effective behaviors gleaned from both elementary and secondary teachers she has read about. She directly teaches new academic terms and models her thinking aloud from a portion of the article. After these introductory activities, the teacher organizes students into groups of five. Each group examines the article for its overall logic, focusing on evaluating the validity of the claim and the relevance and sufficiency of the evidence. Her students use the organizer to record the efforts of their group. There is time near the end of the period for students (as well as the teacher) to read the work of all of the groups. The teacher helps students recap the challenges and successes of their first effort at implementing this technique.

Secondary Nonexample of Judging Reasoning and Evidence

The nonexample secondary teacher is working from the same goal, but is reluctant to consult with her colleagues regarding information and teaching approaches. She is shortchanging her students and short-circuiting her opportunities for becoming a highly effective teacher.

Determining If Students Can Evaluate the Reasoning and Evidence of an Author

Here are some ways that you can monitor if your students are becoming more skilled at evaluating whether an author's reasoning is valid and concurrently whether the author's evidence is relevant and sufficient.

- Collect think sheets and other documents to read what students have written to explain their own thinking.

- Evaluate the types of digital resources students are using to find credible and relevant information and talk students through the reasons they selected a particular source.

- Check whether students are independently examining reasoning.

- Take time to reflect on the quality of the reasoning in group work and listen for suggestions from students about what could help them be more productive.

Use the following student proficiency scale to determine the progression of your students' abilities to judge the validity of author's reasoning as well as the relevance and sufficiency of an author's evidence.

Table 6.5: Student Proficiency Scale for Judging Reasoning and Evidence

Emerging	Fundamental	Desired Result
Students can define the terms *delineate, evaluate, defensible, sufficient,* and *relevant* but cannot identify how these concepts are evident in the work of an author.	Students can identify the concepts that are evident in an author's work but are unable to evaluate the reasoning of the author or the sufficiency and relevance of the evidence.	Students can successfully identify a claim in the work of another person, establish grounds, and provide backing and qualifiers. Students can evaluate the reasoning of the author and the sufficiency and relevance of the evidence.

Scaffold and Extend Instruction to Meet Students' Needs

Meeting the needs of your students may require designing lessons for both your struggling and highest-achieving students to become more self-managed in your classroom. Below are some examples of each:

Scaffolding

- Provide peer support for struggling students.

- Provide scripts for students to use at home to practice the pronunciation and meaning of new academic terms.

- When students are expected to complete all the steps of an organizer independently, provide the claim for struggling students so they can complete the rest of the process.

- Provide written examples and nonexamples to give students more opportunities to understand the process.

Extending

- Have students design or redesign your organizers to offer more information to help struggling students.

- Compare the work of two authors on the same topic to analyze if their claims and evidence have significant similarities or differences. Hypothesize reasons for this.

- Compare an earlier work of an author with a much later one. Analyze how the author's thinking and evidence may have shifted during the passage of time.

Conclusion

The goal of this book is to enable teachers to become more effective in teaching content to their students. The beginning step, as you have learned in the preceding pages, is to become skilled at helping students *examine their reasoning—a two-part strategy that includes examining logic in reasoning and supporting claims with evidence.*

To determine if this goal has been met, you will need to gather information from students, as well as solicit feedback from your supervisor or colleagues, to find someone willing to embark on this learning journey with you. Engage in a meaningful self-reflection on your use of the strategy. If you acquire nothing else from this book, let it be the *importance of monitoring.* The tipping point in your level of expertise and your students' achievement is *monitoring.* Implementing this strategy well is not enough. Your goal is the desired result: evidence that your students have developed a deeper understanding of the content by examining their own reasoning.

To be most effective, view implementation as a three-step process:

1. Implement the strategy using your energy and creativity to adopt and adapt the various techniques in this guide.

2. Monitor for the desired result. In other words, while you are implementing the technique, determine whether that technique is effective with the students.

3. If, as a result of your monitoring, you realize that your instruction was not adequate for students to achieve the desired result, seek out ways to change and adapt.

Although you can certainly experience this guide and gain expertise independently, the process will be more beneficial if you read and work through its contents with colleagues. Use the following reflection and discussion questions during a team meeting or even as food for thought prior to a meeting with your coach, mentor, or supervisor.

Reflection and Discussion Questions

Use the following reflection and discussion questions during a team meeting or even as food for thought prior to a meeting with your coach, mentor, or supervisor:

1. How has your instruction changed as a result of reading and implementing the instructional techniques found in this book?

2. What ways have you found to modify and enhance the instructional techniques found in this book to scaffold and extend your instruction?

3. What was your biggest challenge, in terms of implementing this instructional strategy?

4. How would you describe the changes in your students' learning that have occurred as a result of implementing this instructional strategy?

5. What will you do to share what you have learned with colleagues at your grade level or in your department?

References

Common Core State Standards Initiative. (2010a). *Common Core State Standards for English language arts & literacy in history/social studies, science, and technical subjects*. Washington, DC: Author. Retrieved September 10, 2014, from http://corestandards.org/assets/CCSSI_ELA%20Standards.pdf

Common Core State Standards Initiative. (2010b). *Common Core State Standards for mathematics*. Washington, DC: Author. Retrieved September 10, 2014, from http://www.corestandards.org/wp-content/uploads/Math_Standards.pdf

Dickson, S. V., Collins, V. L., Simmons, D. C., & Kame'enui, E. J. (1998). Metacognitive strategies: Instructional and curricular basics and implications. In D. C. Simmons & E. J. Kame'enui (Eds.), *What reading research tells us about children with diverse learning needs* (pp. 361–380). Hillsdale, NJ: Erlbaum.

Marzano, R. J. (2007). *The art and science of teaching*. Alexandria, VA: Association for Curriculum and Supervision Development.

Marzano, R. J., Boogren, T., Kanold-McIntyre, J., & Pickering, D. (2012). *Becoming a reflective teacher*. Denver, CO: Marzano Research Lab.

Marzano, R. J., & Toth, M. D. (2013). *Deliberate practice for deliberate growth: Teacher evaluation systems for continuous instructional Improvement*. West Palm Beach, FL: Learning Sciences International.

Marzano, R. J., & Toth, M. D. (2014). *Teaching for rigor: A call for a critical instructional shift*. West Palm Beach, FL: Learning Sciences International.

Massachusetts Department of Education. (2003). *History and social science curriculum framework*. Malden, MA: Author. Retrieved September 10, 2014, from http://www.doe.mass.edu/frameworks/hss/final.pdf

McEwan-Adkins, E. K. (2010). *40 reading intervention strategies for K–6 students: Research-based support for RTI*. Bloomington, IN: Solution Tree Press.

McEwan-Adkins, E. K., & Burnett, A. J. (2012). *20 literacy strategies to meet the Common Core: Increasing rigor in middle and high school classrooms*. Bloomington, IN: Solution Tree Press.

NGSS Lead States. (2013). *Next Generation Science Standards: For states, by states*. Washington, DC: National Academies Press. Retrieved October 11, 2013, from http://www.nextgenscience.org/next-generation-science-standards

ProCon.org. (2014). "Climate Change Debate ProCon.org," ProCon.org. Last modified June 27, 2014. http://climatechange.procon.org/

Rittle-Johnson, R., & Star, J. R. (2007). Does comparing solution methods facilitate conceptual and procedural knowledge? An experimental study on learning to solve equations. *Journal of Educational Psychology, 99*(3) 561–574.

Sturges, P. (2002). *The little red hen makes a pizza.* New York: Puffin Books.

Index

C

CCR (College and Career Readiness)
Anchor Standards
 defined, 2
 language of logic, 18
 processing text, 53
 vocabulary for producing and
 defending claims, 52
 vocabulary for reasoning and evidence in an author's work, 75–76
CCSS (Common Core State Standards), 3
 defined, 2
CCSSI (Common Core State Standards
 Initiative), 2
claims, producing and defending
 common mistakes, avoiding, 57
 description of technique, 51
 examples and nonexamples,
 57–62
 implementation, 53–56
 monitoring for desired result,
 62–63
 processing text, 53–54
 scaffolding and extending
 instruction, 63
 student proficiency scale, 63
 vocabulary for, 51–52
claims in an author's work, identifying
 and analyzing
 common mistakes, avoiding,
 67–68
 description of technique, 65
 examples and nonexamples,
 68–73
 implementation, 66–67

 monitoring for desired result,
 73–74
 scaffolding and extending
 instruction, 74
 student proficiency scale, 74
 template for, 66–67
 vocabulary for, 66
compare/contrast approach, 40–41
content
 defined, 2
 identifying and utilizing appropriate, 9

D

desired result
 See also name of instructional
 technique
 defined, 2
 monitoring, 10–11
directly instructing, 7–8
 See also name of instructional
 technique

E

errors and response accuracy
 common mistakes, avoiding,
 31–32
 conclusions, jumping to, 29–30
 description of technique, 29
 examples and nonexamples,
 32–35
 examples for students, providing,
 30–31
 implementation, 29–31

Notes

Notes

Notes

Notes

Notes

MARZANO CENTER

Essentials for Achieving Rigor SERIES

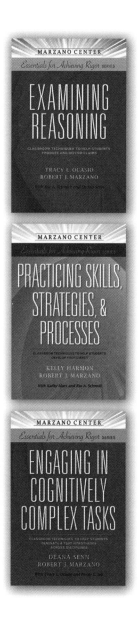

LearningSciencesInternational
LEARNING AND PERFORMANCE MANAGEMENT